NYAYA PANCHAYATS
AS INSTRUMENTS OF JUSTICE

Nyaya Panchayats as Instruments of Justice

S. N. MATHUR

Published for

INSTITUTE OF SOCIAL SCIENCES

by

CONCEPT PUBLISHING COMPANY, NEW DELHI 110 059

The research project: 'Decentralisation of Administration of Justice – Nyaya Panchayats' and this publication were made possible by a grant from: THE FORD FOUNDATION.

ISBN: 81-7022-613-9

First Published in 1997

Published and Printed by
Ashok Kumar Mittal
Concept Publishing Company
A/15-16, Commercial Block, Mohan Garden
NEW DELHI 110 059 (India)

Layout by
Institute of Social Sciences
B-7/18 Safdarjung Enclave
New Delhi 110 029

Foreword

ONE of the major drawbacks of the 73rd Constitution Amendment Act to make Panchayats institutions of self-government was that it did not provide for justice system (Nyaya Panchayats) at the level of district and below. After a study of the Conformity Acts of the states, the Institute of Social Sciences came to the conclusion that the problem of decentralising the administration of justice, both criminal and civil, together with decentralising police administration through the Panchayats was a crucial area which must be studied and brought to national attention. Shri Nirmal Mukarji (former Cabinet Secretary and Governor of Punjab and presently a consultant to the Institute on local government studies) encouraged the Institute to take up this major issue in all earnestness. We were fortunate to get the services of Shri S. N. Mathur for this important study. He dealt with police administration for several decades, having at the end been Director General of Police, Punjab and Director, Intelligence Bureau in the Government of India. This publication is the result of Shri. Mathur's invaluable experience, hard work and extraordinary insights into the problem.

Half way through the study the Institute organised a discussion on the subject in February 1995. A number of distinguished persons in the field of justice systems participated in the meet. Shri Ramakrishna Hegde opened the discussion with his experience in Karnataka and this study benefitted from the deliberations.

While the research was in progress, it was felt that the justice related issues and the decentralisation of police administration through the Panchayats should be dealt with in two stages, without losing sight of the link between them. The forthcoming volume on police administration and panchayati raj will thus be a sequal the present book.

GEORGE MATHEW
Director

1 November 1996

Preface

IN olden times there were traditional panchayats. After independence came panchayats designed as agencies of development. Now there are panchayats constitutionally recognised as institutions of self-government.

The traditional panchayats were autonomous in their limited domain of maintaining harmony in village life and settling disputes. The home-spun justice they dispensed was perhaps more natural than the natural justice of the courts. The agency panchayats were quite different, for their focus was on development and even there they had little autonomy to implement the few schemes assigned to them. Any development they delivered was as instruments of central planning. The constitutional panchayats that have now come into being are, or ought to be, on another plane altogether since their organising principle is self-government.

Self-government implies autonomy and the power to govern in an exclusive area of jurisdiction. As of now the constitutional panchayats have neither autonomy, nor power to govern, nor exclusive jurisdiction. In the absence of these key elements there is no real difference between the new panchayats and the older agency panchayats. So much so that the catch-phrase coined for the earlier lot–Panchayati Raj Institutions, or PRIs, for short–continues to be used freely in both governmental and academic parlance. Clearly, the stranglehold of the past must be broken if the new panchayats are to have the distinguishing characteristic of self-governance intended for them.

Municipalities are in much the same position. Along with panchayats these too were constitutionally defined as institutions of self-government, and are similarly bereft of the key elements of autonomy, governing power and exclusive jurisdiction. The two sets of institutions–panchayats and municipalities–need to be viewed as a new stratum of governance. Henceforth the country is meant, by the Constitution, to be governed by three strata of governance instead of only two: central, state and local. This vision has so far remained unfulfilled because local governance have been given form but not substance.

What should be done to fill form with substance? At one level local governments must organise themselves as an interest group, cutting across state boundaries, to fight for their rights. It is only through sustained political struggle that they will be able to compel the polity, held captive so far by the central and state governments, to yield to them their due by way of autonomy, power and jurisdiction. At another level, there is need for ideational input so that the struggle for local governments' rights has concrete goals before it.

Two goals that have somehow remained outside the ambit of most thinking about local governance are decentralising the system of justice and, parallelling that, decentralising police functioning. There is clearly a linkage between the two. Yet each is an important enough agenda to be dealt with on its own.

Decentralised justice found expression in the concept of *Nyaya Panchayats* incorporated in the panchayat legislation of some states in the past. The Constitutional Amendments that gave birth to the new panchayats and municipalities were, however, completely silent on the subject. Consequently, so were the conformity laws enacted by the states. *Nyaya Panchayats* have thus been wholly eliminated. Very likely this was inadvertently done. Whatever the reason, decentralised justice now needs to be vigorously reviewed, for without a local 'judiciary' local governance will remain glaringly incomplete and the people deprived of the inestimable benefit of justice at their doorstep. The present study aims to do just that to vigorously revive an important but sorely neglected agenda.

The author of the study, Mr. S. N. Mathur, is a distinguished police officer, now retired. For some time he was Punjab's Director-General of Police. At a relatively early age he was appointed Director, Intelligence Bureau of the Government of

India, generally regarded as the topmost post a police officer can aspire to. His professional competence and integrity ensured his continuance as chief of intelligence despite the change of government in 1977. Almost alone among his contemporaries he has steadfastly held the view that police functioning needs to be decentralised, making the local constabulary answerable to local governments. Overcoming his natural reticence he agreed to undertake a thorough study of the subject with the aim of giving practical shape to a decentralised system of policing.

While the design of the study was under discussion the point arose that police decentralization could not be gone into in isolation of judicial decentralisation. Although Mr. Mathur possessed no expertise in this related subject, and said so emphatically, he was persuaded to take up a study of how the administration of justice could be decentralised, bearing in mind the broad objectives of local governance and more especially the objective of decentralising police administration.

Mr. Mathur's study makes refreshing reading. It is neither a dry-as-dust judicial document nor a pedantic academician's thesis. It sets out in plain language a concerned citizen's analysis of the subject and a seasoned administrator's well-judged conclusions and recommendations. Mr. Mathur has adopted the unusual, but extremely helpful, device of quoting extensively from the writings of committees and individuals so that the thinking of these others is readily and fully available. The aim of the study is to generate, or rather to regenerate, discussion and debate on the question of entrusting specified civil and criminal matters exclusively to *Nyaya Panchayats*. To the extent it succeeded in doing so, it will prove to be a useful ideational input for the substance that local governance needs.

After commencing the study Mr. Mathur suffered a setback in his health. That caused some delay. But it speaks volumes for the author's courage and tenacity of purpose that he did not give up and, despite severe handicaps, has not only completed this study successfully but is all set to get on to the study close to his rich experience, the decentralisation of police functioning. I far more keenly look forward to the outcome of that study.

This work owes a great deal to the unfailing support extended by the Institute of Social Sciences, New Delhi and more so to the personal interest of its dynamic Director, Dr. George Mathew.

17 May, 1996 NIRMAL MUKARJI

Acknowledgement

I AM most indebted to the reports of Justice Bhagwati Committee on Judicare, Justice Krishna Iyer Committee on Legal Aid, also Justice Krishna Iyer's collection of lectures and essays entitled *Of Law and Life*, in addition to the reports of the Law Commission and in particular, to the report of the Study Team presided by Shri Rajgopaul. These reports gave me an insight into the working of Judiciary in India. A number of valuable field studies have been made by some scholars. In view of my inability to actually visit the rural areas and study on the spot, the functioning of *Nyaya Panchayats*, I have heavily borrowed from the studies made by Mr M. K. Khan and Smt Kamlesh Sharma (both of Sagar University, Madhya Pradesh) from their monograph entitled, "Profile of a Nyaya Panchayat"; Dr R. Kushwaha's, "A case study of Varanasi District"; the joint study of Shri M.V. Mathur, Shri Iqbal Narain and Shri V. M. Sinha entitled, "A Study of Nyaya Panchayats in Rajasthan"; the study entitled, "Politics of Informal Justice", conducted by Mr. Richard L. Abel of the University of California. I am extremely grateful to Dr Upendra Baxi for reproducing his address entitled, "Critique of Nyaya Panchayats in Karnataka" and to Shri K. S. Krishnaswamy, for his article, "Karnataka's New Steps Backwards". I am also grateful to Dr Jose P. Verghese. His paper entitled, "Empowering the villages with a Dispute Settlement System", I found scholarly throwing light *inter alia* on ancient history of the *Panchayat System*.

Finally, I shall be failing in my duty if I do not thank profusely, Shri Nirmal Mukarji for his guidance and Dr George Mathew for his cooperation, at every step.

My thanks are also due to Shri Rajagopal, my research assistant who has been extremely helpful throughout.

S. N. MATHUR

Acknowledgement

Contents

Contents

Part I

Chapter 1

Introduction

JUSTICE and the rule of law for the millions residing in the rural areas of our country remains a painful illusion. The existing judicial system is neither accessible nor capable of delivering quick justice, apart from the forbidding cost involved, for the poor in the rural areas.

A forum for the resolution of disputes with people's participation in the administration of justice is the constitutional goal enunciated in Article 39A. Whereas, Article 40 directs the state to take steps to organize Village Panchayats and endow them with such power and authority as to enable them to function as units of self-government. As also pointed out by Gandhiji at a prayer meeting, "In the true democracy of India, the unit was the village. Even if one village wanted Panchayati Raj which was called republic in English, no one could stop it. True democracy could not be worked by 20 men sitting at the centre. It had to be worked from below by the people of every village."

The Constitution (73rd Amendment) enjoined that there shall be a Gram Sabha in each village exercising such powers and performing such functions at the village level as the legislation of a state may provide by law. Further, Panchayats should be constituted in every state at the village, intermediate and district levels, thus bringing about uniformity in the *Panchayati Raj* structure. Unfortunately, in this amendment there was no mention of decentralisation of justice and no state legislation in the wake of this amendment, took up this subject.

The Institute of Social Sciences took the initiative to study the subject of decentralisation of administration of justice including judiciary and police. The primary step in respect of decentralisation of judiciary was to organise an institution at the village level to function as a forum for resolving disputes and deal with petty cases of civil and criminal nature to provide justice at the doorstep, to the villagers. Against this background, preparation of a book on *Nyaya Panchayats* was entrusted to me.

In this book, I have tried to establish that down the course of history, the *Nyaya Panchayats*, have provided access to justice to the rural India, through the process of participatory justice. With the arrival of the British, the Anglo-Saxon system had taken this advantage away from the rural poor and to a large extent the same situation obtains even today.

In my view, it should be possible to design and develop, a model framework of the institution of *Nyaya Panchayats*, administering justice at the village level, in the spirit of the past traditions, keeping in view, the socio-economic developments and also in consonance with the constitutional mandate.

The subject of *Nyaya Panchayats*, however, raises a host of pertinent questions–How should the *Nyaya Panchayats* be constituted? What kind of qualifications should govern the selection/election of members of a *Nyaya Panchayat*? What procedures should be adopted by the *Nyaya Panchayats*? Should they be bound by formal legal procedures or left to deal with cases before them through rules of fairness, natural justice and conscience? Should these *Nyaya Panchayats* be activists in the performance of their role or play the passive role in the Anglo-American tradition? What kind of training and orientation courses be arranged for the members of a *Nyaya Panchayat*? What jurisdiction and powers be vested in the *Nyaya Panchayats*? These are only some of the more significant issues to be tackled.

During the course of this study, I shall endeavour to deal with all questions relating to the constitution of *Nyaya Panchayats*, the mode of selection of *panchs*, their jurisdiction and mode of functioning and a host of related issues.

This book is in two parts. Part I deals with the need for

reform in the judicial system and the *Nyaya Panchayats* in a historical perspective. Part II, deals with an appraisal of the working of the *Nyaya Panchayats* in the past and touching a dividend on the same, what should be the model framework of a present-day *Nyaya Panchayat*.

It is likely that some experts may have views different from those expressed in this book, particularly in the design of a model framework for *Nyaya Panchayats*. I shall only be too happy to receive their views, opinions and criticism.

Chapter 2

Need for Reform of Judicial System

THE restructuring of judicial system at the grassroots level should be an essential part of effective legal services programme. The entire object is to bring justice nearer to people, particularly those living in our villages, mostly backward and indigent. The existing situation of the legal and judicial system in the rural areas is best brought out by Justice P. N. Bhagwati Committee on Judicare, constituted by the Government of India, which submitted its report in 1977. The following observations of the Committee are worthy of consideration:

> "To-day the poor and the disadvantaged are cut off from the legal system–they are functional outlaws not only because they are priced out of judicial system by reason of its expensiveness and dilatoriness but also because of the nature of the legal and judicial system. They have distrust and suspicion of the law, the law courts and the lawyers for several reasons. One is ignorance and illiteracy on their part which prevents them from taking advantage of the legal process. Another is their helplessness and lack of assertiveness which arises by reason of social disabilities and economic dependence and that also places the legal process effectively beyond their reach. But apart from these factors which we have discussed at length in another part of the Report, the functioning of the courts is unfortunately shrouded in mystery for the poor and the under-privileged. There is an air of excessive formalism in law courts which overawes them and sometimes scares them. Often the proceedings are conducted in a language which they do not understand. They do not know what is happening in the court. They sit as helpless spectators, not understanding what is going on in the court in regard to their own case. It is an ironical situation that they who should know most about their case know the least. They are completely mystified by the

court proceedings and this, to a large extent, alienates them from the legal and judicial process. And lastly our system of administration of justice, which is an inheritance from the British, is archaic and suffers from obsolescence and obscurantism. It is not at all adapted to our socio-economic conditions and is wholly unsuited to our national genius. The result is that it has failed to inspire confidence in the poor and they have little faith in its capacity to do justice."

Inadequacy of Our Judicial System

Our legal and judicial system is not adequate to meet the need of the new society. It is not sufficiently responsive to the new norms and values which are replacing the old and does not reflect properly and adequately the new approach, which characterizes the true purposes and functions of law. The judicial system, therefore, needs to be reformed so that it becomes more suited to the new socio-economic conditions and becomes an effective instrument of delivering justice to poor and disadvantaged. It thus becomes imperative to consider what changes should be made in our judicial system so that the new system is capable of serving the poor and backward villagers and not only the privileged class.

Justice, according to Justice Bhagwati, "denotes social and economic justice, apart from individual conflict resolution, based on legal norms. It connotes programmes and developmental strategies aimed at India's metamorphosis into a contented society, ready to involve all its citizens in the pursuit of happiness. Today, for the vast millions of our people, justice is a cynical phrase, a painful illusion. The soul of good government is justice to the people and that is why the preamble to our Constitution highlights it in its triple respects, namely political, social and economic as a promise and process. The question naturally arises how can we redeem this tryst with justice on behalf of our teeming millions in rags, tatters and tears. The success of any project consists of scientific planning. Therefore, we in India need a new legal technology, new judicature models and men, a development and remedy oriented jurisprudence and judicare project that is designed as a pressure and potent delivery system of law and justice to the people in rural remoteness. If we want distributive justice to become a reality for those who now share stark deprivation and poverty, one of the basics should be, easy access to institutions of justice through village level delivery of justice. Having regard to the smallness of the subject matter of village litigation and the considerable bad blood that may be generated by cantankerous and unproductive legal battles and remembering that petty cases are mostly those, where at least one party is a small man, we must create mini courts which save the poor from the litigiousness".

It is common knowledge that a litigation, civil or criminal, whichever party wins or loses, leaves a trail of bitterness and bad blood and tremendous financial loss for both, apart from protracted trials and resulting frustration. In Indian conditions, law and justice at the *Panchayat* level with a conciliatory methodology is an imperative necessity. This can only be achieved by having a suitable forum for conciliation and adjudication involving little cost and no delay with an informal procedure conforming only to the requirements of natural justice where the key word would be justice rather than law. *Nyaya Panchayats* at the village level is the only answer.

Nyaya Panchayats

The institution of *Nyaya Panchayats* is indeed one of the oldest institution in the country. Reference to *Nyaya Panchayats* abound in ancient literature and historical accounts. The *Nyaya Panchayat* in the earliest available accounts, were creations of villages themselves and were composed of persons who were generally respected and to whose decisions the villagers were accustomed to unqualified obedience. The *Nyaya Panchayat* exercised great measure of authority and commanded willing allegiance of the people. The *Nyaya Panchayat* played an important role in solving disputes of the village. "Sitting on the *Panchayat*, the elders of the village used to solve disputes arising between the members of the village community. These elders used to live in the villages themselves and were by virtue of their residence well acquainted with local conditions and

knew the habits, customs and practices of the people. Almost all individuals of the village were known to them. In view of all these factors they easily came to know reasons behind the disputes that arose. They heard the parties in the presence of the entire village and solved the disputes. Public opinion of the village used to act as a powerful influence on the parties to the disputes and because justice was meted out at the very place where the dispute took place, it used to be inexpensive and immediate. One direct advantage of this was that normally no attempt was made to fabricate false evidence and even if an attempt was made the same could be easily demolished. When the village elders took over on themselves the duty of solving problems, it used to have a salutary effect on both sides and disputes and quarrels arising out of groupism used to come to an end and not drag on. In fact, all used to have faith and trust in the village elders which gave them strength to solve dispute objectively and impartially."*

Thus *Panchayat* justice is not a novel idea but a time-honoured institution having its deep roots in the ethos of the country. It is village self-government in action at the level of administration of justice. It both helped in involvement of people in dealing with law and justice and institutionalization of expeditious local resolution of disputes.

Ideological Justification for Nyaya Panchayats

There is also an ideological justification for *Nyaya Panchayat* since that makes for democratic decentralisation and people's involvement in one of the most important branches of governance–the dispensation of justice. It was Mahatma Gandhi who first saw the great potentiality of reviving the system of village justice at the time of non-cooperation movement in 1920-21, when he advocated boycott of law courts, he made the setting up of *Panchayat* in villages for settling disputes, a fighting militant slogan. He passionately believed in the ideal of self-sufficient village community and observed in the issue of

* Report of the Committee set up by the Congress Working Committee, 1954.

Harijan, dated 22 July 1946, "the Gram Panchayat shall be entrusted with dispensation of the justice, no separate judicial Panchayats are necessary. The poor peasant need not go out of his village, spend his hard earned money and waste weeks and months in towns in litigation. He can get all the necessary witnesses in the village and fight out his own case without being exploited by the lawyers. When intricate points of law arise, sub judge from the taluka or district could come down to the village and assist the panchayat in deciding difficult cases. The sub judge shall also act as a guide, friend and philosopher to the ignorant villagers by acquainting them with the laws of the state. Such a judicial system will not only be simple, prompt and cheap, but also just."

Nyaya Panchayat would be able to remove many of the defects of the British system of administration of the justice, since they would be manned by people who would have knowledge of local customs and habits, attitudes and values and who would be familiar with the ways of thought and living of the parties before them. Drastically low cost informal procedure, absence of technicalities, nearness, both geographical and psychological, community of shared attitudes and values and greater scope for compromise, would be some of the definite advantages of the system of *Nyaya Panchayats* and they would make the system of administration of justice more relevant and meaningful to the poor masses and thereby generate greater confidence in them. The poor would feel that the authority which is administering justice to them is their own and is not a part of an alien system which neither understands nor trusts.

Chapter 3

Nyaya Panchayats : A Historical Perspective

THE administration of justice by *Village Panchayat* and concomitant participation of the people in the administration of justice in India are as old as the villages themselves. Though there is some difference of opinion on the point whether or not *Panchayats* in ancient India were truly representative bodies and had legal sanction, there is considerable unanimity on the point that the *Panchayat* as an agency for settling local disputes belongs to antiquity. A number of historical accounts and legends lend support to this view point.

Traditional Courts : Ancient India

The ancient philosopher-theologist, Narad, indicates four types of traditional courts of adjudication, viz. the family, the occupational group, the clan and the king. Yagnavalkya also assigns to the king the responsibility of promoting the legal system supported by the five pillars of the family, caste, occupational group, the clan, and the village. Additionally, the king is charged with the responsibility that these socio-legal entities observe their respective duties conscientiously. He mentions three courts of adjudicature, viz. *kula*, *sreni* and *puga*. Ordinarily, in the matter of deciding disputes, each successive court is superior to the previous one. It would be a useful exercise to elaborate on the classification by Yagnavalkya. Broadly speaking the *kula* (*Panchayat* of family/relatives) is the lowest court and is composed of kinsmen having the right to decide on small matters concerning members of the *kula*. The *sreni* (the *Panchayat* of the members of the same occupational group) is the next higher court, having jurisdiction over traders, artisans, and the like, pursuing similar or related means of livelihood. Often the *sreni* had jurisdiction over the members of different castes too. The *puga* (the *Panchayat* of different castes within a given territory, say a village) is a court having jurisdiction over members of different castes and occupations, inhabitants of the same village or town. There are indications that these *Panchayats* were independent in their working. Though the king encouraged and organized these *Panchayats* and guided them, he seldom interfered with their working. From the writings of Yagnavalkya it is amply brought out that the directives issued by the king to these *Panchayats* used to be based on tradition, the rule of law and were not governed by his personal whims and fancies. Further, the king used to act as a guardian of these *Panchayats* so much so that the faltering *Panchayats* were taken to task by the king.

Jurisdiction of Traditional Courts

About the qualifications for the membership of these courts, the ancient law givers lay down that they be well versed in Vedic *dharma*, self controlled, well born, noble and selfless, experienced and capable. The members of these *Panchayats* were considered the best judges of the merits of a case as they lived in that very place where a given dispute arose. The *Panchayat* had jurisdiction over almost every type of dispute arising in the village community. They decided both civil and criminal matters and their powers ordinarily were not confined to cases within any financial limit. The fact that the members of the courts came from the very village had a salutary effect on the litigants. These *Panchayats* have also been mentioned by *Kautilya* in *Arthashastra*. These continued to function with minor variations till the advent of the Muslim rule in India, which made substantial in-roads into the *Panchayat* system prevailing at that time.

Courts during the Muslim and British Rule

The Muslim rulers constituted courts of judicature which were at variance with the traditional system. *Ghaziz*, *Muftis* and *Mir Adils* were appointed to dispense justice. However, these mostly functioned at the district level or above, leaving the village level mostly untouched. Thus by accident or design, the *Village Panchayat* in the country continued to function relatively undisturbed. However, during the reign of certain Muslim kings like Sher Shah and Akbar, the *Panchayat* system received moral and administrative support to a great extent. Then, there were also a number of feudal territories, where in the villages, the *Panchayat* systems continued to operate undisturbed. These *Panchayats* suffered decline in their jurisdiction and authority with the downfall of the Mughal rule in India. The downfall was further accelerated by the change in administrative policy introduced by the East India Company and eventually the British Government. The British set up courts for adjudicating civil and criminal cases. These courts almost stifled people's participation in the administration of justice as these were solely manned by bureaucrats. On the other hand, when people saw that the power of the state was behind the newly established courts and not behind the ancient *Panchayat* institutions, they naturally abandoned the old courts and turned to the new ones. While there was a strong feeling among the officers of the East India Company against the institution of the *Panchayat* in ordinary disputes but their usefulness in the determination of purely social questions such as those relating to caste and of revenue matters, was recognized. Even Elphinston asserted in 1821 that, *"our principle instrument should continue to be the Panchayat and must be exempted from all forms of interference and new regulations"*. Even under the British rule a few provinces tried the experiment of incorporating the institution of the *Panchayat* by law into the regular judicial system. The earliest to start was the Madras Presidency when a regulation was passed in 1816 permitting trial of cases by *panchs*. The regulation was passed with a view to diminish the expense on litigation and render the principal and more intelligent inhabitants, useful and respectable, by employing them for administering justice to their neighbours. Nevertheless, *Village Panchayats* and *Nyaya Panchayats* fell prey to official indifference and in most provinces became defunct, despite the fact that the Royal Commission on decentralisation strongly recommended the revival of *Village Panchayat* as the lowest unit of local self-government. It suggested that, *"Panchayat should have civil and criminal jurisdiction in petty cases arising within the village"*.

Indian Police Commission (1902)

The Indian Police Commission of 1902 observed that, *"it is expedient to relegate the trial of petty offences to the village headmen and the Panchayats and where the system does not exist it shall be cautiously and experimentally introduced"*. This recommendation was not followed and implemented effectively and in course of time the regular judiciary was saddled with the growing volume of cases which ultimately resulted in delay and in a large number of cases, even denial of justice.

Similarly, in 1915 the Government of India suggested the establishment of *Nyaya Panchayats* and the matter was entrusted to the state governments. In 1920, the Bombay *Village Panchayat* Act was passed which saw the creation of a large number of *Panchayati Adalats* with certain powers relating to the administration of civil and criminal justice. It must be pointed out here that the idea of investing an elected body of the villagers with judicial powers, was strongly opposed by the select committee of the Legislative Council. In the mean time the workload of the courts, civil and judicial went on mounting. At this stage the Civil Justice Committee of 1924-25 endorsed what some of the earlier committees and Police Commission had suggested. In the view of the Civil Justice Committee "the *Village Panchayats*, the villagers mediating between contending parties in their own villages have in some form or the other existed in the country from the earliest times and that too without resort to any elaborate complicated machinery. The judicial work of the *Panchayats* is part of that village system which in most parts of India and Burma have been the basis of indigenous administration from times immemorial."

The Bombay Nyaya Panchayats

It was under the Bombay *Village Panchayat* Act 1937 that judicial powers were entrusted to a village *Nyaya Panchayat* which consisted partly of elected members of the *Panchayat* and partly outsiders. The idea of *Nyaya Panchayat* even in the pre-independence period attracted the attention of the national leaders directing the freedom struggle. They favoured

Panchayati Raj as a means to curb the excessive indulgence of the villagers in litigation which was telling heavily on the peace and prosperity of the country-side. It was felt that *Nyaya Panchayat* as part of the *Panchayati Raj* could render the administration of justice speedy, inexpensive and effective, and hence limit the quantum of strife and litigation in the village. However, *Nyaya Panchayat* as well as *Village Panchayat*, in the Bombay Presidency as elsewhere, oscillated between official indifference and neglect for quite some time.

Towards the revival of *Nyaya Panchayat*, definite steps were taken only after India attained independence. One of the directive principles of the Constitution lays down that the state governments should organise *Village Panchayats* with such powers and authority as may be necessary to enable them to function as units of self-government.

Balwantrai Mehta Report

The Balwantrai Mehta Study Team was appointed in 1957 to study Community Development and National Extension Services Programme specially from the point of view of assessing the extent of popular participation and to recommend the creation of institutions through which such participation can be achieved. It recommended the constitution of statutory elective bodies with the necessary resources, power and authority, devolved on them and a decentralised administrative system, working under their control. This study team also recommended that the basic unit of democratic decentralisation should be located at the block and *samiti* level. The study team envisaged directly elected *Panchayat* for a village or a group of villages, an executive body called *Panchayat Samiti* for a block which directly elected and co-opted members and advisory body called the *Zilla Parishad* at the district level constituted indirectly mainly through ex-officio members from the lower tier and others with the Collector as the Chairman. Based on the broad suggestions of the study team most of the country was covered with *Panchayati Raj Institutions* in the succeeding decades.

Asoka Mehta Committee

The Asoka Mehta Committee gave its report to the Government of India in August 1978 on the working of *Panchayati Raj Institutions*. It recommended a two-tier setup–district level and *mandal* level, covering the population of 15,000 to 20,000 and suggested the abolition of blocks as units of administration. The Committee also suggested holding of regular elections, compulsory items of taxation in their jurisdiction and transfer of land revenue collection to them. It also felt that a constitutional provision was necessary to strengthen the *Panchayati Raj Institutions*. This Committee also dealt with the subject of *Nyaya Panchayats* and expressed the view that a qualified judge should preside over the *Nyaya Panchayat* and elected *Nyaya panchs* should be associated with it.

The 14th Law Commission

The 14th Law Commission rendered yeoman's service in making comprehensive recommendations after review of the existing *Panchayat* courts.

The important conclusions reached by the Law Commission may be enumerated as follows:

- *Panchayat* courts are capable of doing a good deal of useful work by relieving the regular courts of petty civil litigation and criminal cases of the simpler types.

- The *Panchayats*, as compared to the ordinary courts, are in a position to dispose of simple cases, more cheaply and expeditiously and with less inconvenience to all concerned.

- An effort should be made to establish and popularize *Panchayat* courts in states where they are not formally established.

- Wherever possible, a *Panchayat* court should be constituted for a group of villages situated in a contiguous area.

- *Nyaya panchs* should be nominated by suitable authority out of those elected *panchs* who possess certain prescribed qualifications like literacy.

- In order to provide continuity, the terms of office of *Nyaya Panchayats* should be staggered.

- The *Panchs* of the *Nyaya Panchayats* should be given training before they are allowed to exercise judicial functions.

- To get over the difficulty caused by the existence of factions, the *panchs* deciding a case might be required to belong to a neighbouring village, or each party to a dispute may be allowed to select his *panch*.

- The jurisdiction of *Panchayat* courts should be exclusive.

- Nature of cases (civil) and the list of offences (criminal) triable by these courts are set out at length in the various state enactments and do not call for any enlargement.

- The criminal jurisdiction of *Panchayat* courts should be limited to inflicting a fine of Rs. 50. They should not have the power to award sentence of imprisonment either substantively, or in default of payment of fine or to bind over parties to keep the peace. Cases in which such action is necessary should be made over to the regular courts.

- The court fee, if any, levied by the *Panchayat* courts should be nominal.

- *Panchayat* courts should not be bound by procedural codes or by the law of evidence.

- *Panchayat* courts should, wherever, possible seek to effect an amicable settlement between the parties.

- Legal practitioners should not be permitted to appear in these courts.

- A revision should lie from the decisions of the *Panchayat* courts in civil and criminal matters to the *munsif* or sub-divisional magistrate, who should be empowered to transfer a case from one *Panchayat* court to another or to the regular court for trial.

- The power of revision should not be given to the District Judge nor should a right of appeal to a larger *Panchayat* be allowed.

- The District Judge should be empowered to direct the removal of *panchs* if he is satisfied that the *panch* in question has been guilty of misconduct in the discharge of his judicial functions. There should be a provision for an appeal against such order of removal.

- A special officer or special officers should be appointed for the purpose of imparting training to *panchs* and to supervise the administration of *Panchayat* courts.

- More detailed information should be collected and published regarding the working of the *Panchayat* courts.

In 1959 in the course of a discussion in the Rajya Sabha on the aforementioned report of the Law Commission, Shri A.K. Sen, the then Law Minister observed, "there is no doubt that the system of justice which obtains today is too expensive for the common man. The small disputes must necessarily be left to be decided by a system of *Panchayat* justice–call it the people's court, call it anything–but it would certainly be subject to such safeguards as we may devise–the only means by which for ordinary disputes at the village level, the common man can be assured by a system of judicial administration which would not be too expensive for him and would not be too dilatory for him".

The Rajagopaul Study Team

The above considerations led to the appointment of a Study Team headed by Shri G. R. Rajagopaul the then Special Secretary (Law), to examine the question of composition, jurisdiction and functions of *Panchayat* courts. The Rajagopaul Study Team gave its report in April 1962. The important issues raised in this report may be mentioned below:

Recommendations of Rajagopaul Study Team

- *Nyaya Panchayats* are of respectable antiquity and success in the past is a clear indication that by reviving and moulding them on the right lines, we will be taking a much needed step in the direction of making law and administration of justice reflect the spirit of the people and become rooted once again in the people.

- A study of the participation of laymen in the administration of justice in some of the leading countries of the world clearly reveals that with appropriate safeguards, it would not be difficult to make an institution of lay judges successful if the need for it is there.

- *Nyaya Panchayats*, wherever they are in existence, are serving a real felt need of the villages by disposing of cases more expeditiously and with minimum of inconvenience and expenses to parties. Although some of the criticism directed against the *Nyaya Panchayat* may be justified, it is possible by suitable safeguards to remove the basis for any such criticisms.

- To avoid the baneful effects of factions, unhealthy rivalries, etc. a *Nyaya Panchayat* may be set up for a group of villages, and the grouping may be made having regard to factors like area, population, contiguity compactness, means of communication, etc. Where, in view of the size and population of a village, a separate *Nyaya Panchayat* has to be set up, the device of splitting the village into a number of wards can be adopted.

- As to the method of constitution of *Nyaya Panchayats*, the system of nomination in any form has to be ruled out. Villages must be given a free hand and the choice lies between the system of direct elections and indirect elections.

The method of indirect elections seems to afford for the time being the best solution and of the various possible methods of indirect elections, the best seems to be the type in which each of the *Gram Panchayats* in the *Nyaya Panchayat* circle elect a specified number of persons to serve on the *Nyaya Panchayat.*

– A minimum age of 30 years and ability to read and write the regional language fluently, may be prescribed as qualifications for a person to be eligible to serve as a *nyaya panch.* No property qualification need be prescribed. Relaxation of this minimum qualification may be necessary in backward areas.

– The jurisdiction of *Nyaya Panchayats* should be exclusive.

– *Nyaya Panchayats* may be given criminal Jurisdiction in respect of petty matters where the punishment in the form of a fine would be an adequate corrective.

– *Nyaya Panchayats* may be empowered to inflict a fine upto Rs. 50. The maximum limit of Rs. 50 may be increased to Rs. 100 if any state government feels justified in doing so. *Nyaya Panchayats* should, however, not be given power to award imprisonment either substantively or in default of payment of fine.

– *Nyaya Panchayats* should not be bound by the procedural codes or the Indian Evidence Act. *Nyaya Panchayat* procedure should be of a simple character but care should be taken to see that principles of natural justice are compiled with.

– No legal practitioner should be allowed to appear before *Nyaya Panchayats*.

– Special officers or specified judicial officers may be appointed in consultation with the High Court, wherever necessary, to supervise and guide the work of *Nyaya Panchayats*.

- It is not necessary to make any provision for appeal from the decisions of *Nyaya Panchayats*.

- Revision should lie from the decisions of *Nyaya Panchayats* to a senior judicial officer. The revisional authority may interfere only if he is not satisfied as to the correctness, legality or propriety of the decision and should refrain from interfering, if he is satisfied that substantive justice has been done.

- No salary or remuneration may be paid to *Nyaya Panchs*, but they should be reimbursed in respect of travelling and other out of pocket expenses.

- *Nyaya panchs* should be accorded the status and protection due to them as members of a judicial body and should be treated as "public servants". All official agencies, particularly police should extend the fullest cooperation to them.

Performance of Nyaya Panchayats

In course of time *Nyaya Panchayat*s were constituted in 15 states by special legislation. However, actual functioning was confined to some states only. In some states the regular *Gram Panchayat* were vested with the judicial functions in addition to executive and municipal functions. In some states the provisions of the *Panchayat* Act, relating to *Nyaya Panchayat* were either held in abeyance or never implemented. Some states abolished these institutions after they had function for some time. In some states *Panchayati Raj Institutions* were not set up at all.

The various committees appointed by the state government to evaluate the working of the *Nyaya Panchayat*s presented a discouraging picture. The Orissa Committee (1958) found that the *Adalati Panchayat* established itself only as "compromising body". The Badal Team of Punjab (1969) felt that judicial functions be withdrawn from *Gram Panchayat*s to enable them to perform their regular functions better. Maharashtra Evaluation Committee (1971) felt that the entrustment of the judicial functions to the *Panchayat* court "on the basis of democratic elections or otherwise are both out of place and unworkable" and felt that *Nyaya Panchayats* were languishing for want of funds, secretarial assistance, lack of powers and people's faith and should be abolished.

The National Police Commission during its tours in the states had discussion with a wide cross-section of the people as also the services, got the impression that working of *Nyaya Panchayats*, though well conceived in principle, suffered in practice mainly because of the lay members being subjected to local influences and pressures and that *Panchayat*s solely comprising lay members were unable to handle the judicial work with requisite attention to the minimum requirements of a judicial process. It was further mentioned that *Nyaya Panchayat*s would function far more effectively if they were manned by trained persons with a certain minimum knowledge of law, rules and procedures. The recommendation of the National Police Commission was that, "the courts proposed at the grassroot level may be called *Gram Nyayalayas* avoiding any reference to *Panchayat* as such so that they may not be viewed as an adjunct or extension of the *Panchayats* which are totally executive bodies with which political functionaries are associated". *Gram Nyayalaya*, according to the National Police Commission, shall be made up of three members. One shall be a presiding judge to be appointed by the district judge from retired judicial officers or other retired government officers who from their experience while in service, would have acquired the requisite knowledge of law and minimum requirements of judicial processes. Two other members of the *Gram Nyayalayas* shall be lay members, appointed by the district judge from a panel of names prepared by the local elected bodies that goes by the name of *Panchayat samiti/Panchayat* union/block committee or its equivalent.

There has been a great emphasis by various committees and commissions for giving the *Panchayati Raj Institutions*, a constitutional status. The Constitution (64th Amendment) Bill 1989 and the Constitution (74th Amendment) Bill 1990, both unfortunately lapsed.

The Constitution (73rd Amendment) Act

The Constitution (73rd Amendment) Bill was introduced in 1991 and passed by both Houses of Parliament. It emerged as Constitution (73rd amendment) Act 1993 and came into force with effect from 24th April 1993. The salient provisions of the Act are as follows:

(i) *Panchayats* will be institutions of self-government.

(ii) There shall be a Gram Sabha in each village exercising such powers and performing such functions at the village level as the legislation of a state may provide by law.

(iii) *Panchayats* shall be constituted in every state at the village, intermediate and district levels, thus bringing about uniformity in the *Panchayati Raj* structure. However, states having a population not exceeding 20 lakhs have been given the option of not having single *Panchayat* at the intermediate level.

(iv) While the elections in respect of all the members in the *Panchayats* at all levels will be direct, the elections of the post of chairperson at the intermediate and district levels will be indirect. The mode of elections of chairpersons at the village level has been left to the state governments to decide.

(v) Reservation of seats for SC/STs has been provided in proportion to their population at each level. Not less than one-third of the total membership has been reserved for women and these seats may be allotted by rotation to different constituencies in a *Panchayat*. Similar reservation has been made in respect of the office of the chairperson also.

(vi) The Act provides for uniform five-year term for *Panchayati Raj Institutions*. In the event of supersession, election to constitute the body should be completed before the expiry of six months from the date of dissolution.

(vii) The state legislative has been given the power to authorise the *Panchayat* to levy, collect and appropriate suitable local taxes and also provide for making grants-in-aid to the *Panchayats* from the consolidated funds of the state. In addition, a Finance Commission has to be constituted once every five years to review the financial position of the *Panchayats* and to make suitable recommendations to the state on the distribution of funds between the state and the local bodies. The Central Finance Commission shall also suggest measures necessary to augment the consolidated fund of a state to supplement the resources for the *Panchayats* in the state. Thus, a large amount of assured funds will flow to the *Panchayati Raj Institutions* which in turn will strengthen people's involvement in the planning process.

(viii) Besides providing for finance, the Act also indicates a set of items in the 11th Schedule of the Constitution which may be entrusted to the *Panchayats* in addition to other schemes for economic development and social justice by state governments.

(ix) To ensure continuity, it has been provided in the Act that all the *Panchayats* existing immediately before the commencement of the amendment act, will continue, until the expiry of their duration, unless dissolved by resolution to that effect passed by the legislative assembly of a state. The state legislatures have also been given time upto a maximum of one year from the commencement of this amendment to bring in necessary amendments to their *Panchayat* acts, so as to conform to the provisions contained in the Constitution.

A Critique of Constitution (73rd Amendment) Act

The Constitution (73rd Amendment) Act had a mixed reception. Mr N.K. Mukarji, an authority on the subject of decentralisation, was not sure whether there is requisite sanction in the Constitutional Amendment to enforce its provisions. If *Panchayati Raj* has to be enforced, would it be infused with the right spirit?. Basically, is a constitutional provision an adequate substitute for political will? Further, is implementing decentralisation below the state level desirable through a constitutional amendment? Whether adopting centralist means will not vitiate the intended ends? Is it desirable to ram down the state downwards decentralisation by constitutional fiat from Delhi "Is acceptability at the receiving end not a relevant factor at all. Should the whole question of decentralisation below the state level not be left entirely to the states".

Mr. Mukarji is keen to know, will the enactment of 73rd Amendment not amount to perpetrating one of the worst features of centralism namely thrusting a uniform prescription on states which are widely disparate in administrative culture, in historical background and in demographic size. With reference to the proposed Part IX for "*The Panchayats*", why should all states be bound to have direct elections for the intermediate level, if any, but be free to choose any type of election at the district level? "The proposed Part IX seems, in some ways, to be a more detailed imposition of 'unitary' India on 'federal' Bharat at the *Panchayat* level, than Part VI already is at the State level."

One aspect of the amendment which came in for universal criticism is the 11th Schedule. According to Mr. L. C. Jain, "It is not a Schedule comparable to the other ten Schedules of the Constitution". The other ten demarcate functions between the Centre and the States, specify concurrent list, and the rights of scheduled areas. There is some specific purpose to them. If one reads the reference to the 11th Schedule in the body of the Amendment, it says, "Schemes under subjects which are listed in the 11th Schedule may be entrusted by the state governments to the *Panchayats*". That is, it does not confer any entitlement or rights/authority on the *Panchayat* over certain specified subjects. But rather, that the *Panchayats* can be appointed as brokers of various departments of the central/state government at the latter's sweet will, to run some scheme which they have devised on their behalf. "Do we need to put something in the Constitution that is so trivial, irrelevant and meaningless"?

Finally, a major lacunae in the 73rd Amendment is the contradictory and inconsistent approach to the idea that the *Panchayats* are institutions of self-government. The Bill had rightly defined the *Panchayat* as an institution of self-government but later in defining the functions of the institution, had narrowed them down to development functions. Without policing (law and order) as a function at each level, no institution of self-government is worth the name.

In the evolution of local government in the country, Lord Ripon had played a major role. It was during his vice-royalty in 1882 that a resolution providing for local boards comprising elected non-official members was passed. Thus the journey, from the idea of a local self-government conceived by Lord Ripon to the "institutions of self-government" enunciated in the 73rd Amendment, took more than a century. This evolution in the federal polity of our country is significant.

Part II

Chapter 4

Functioning of Nyaya Panchayats : Post-Independence Era

IT will be a useful exercise to study the working of *Nyaya Panchayats* in various states where they had been functioning under the state laws enacted from 1950 onwards. It would have been ideal if an empirical study was made on the ground, for the purpose. However, the 73rd Constitutional Amendment led to new enactments in respect of *Panchayati Raj Institutions*. Since our principle object is to put forward a model framework of *Nyaya Panchayats* as a first essential step in the scheme of democratic decentralisation in the light of new developments, the idea of an empirical study was abandoned.

A number of experts have made a study in the field of the functioning of the *Nyaya Panchayats*. These studies provide very useful information in respect of the virtues and shortcomings of *Nyaya Panchayats* in various states, the public response and impact on the administration of justice. We have in these studies, extremely useful material for our present essay. We have selected field studies conducted in three states, viz. Uttar Pradesh, Rajasthan and Karnataka.

Dr. R. Kushwaha, made an in-depth study of the functioning of the *Nyaya Panchayats* in the Varanasi district under the aegis of the Institute of Constitutional and Parliamentary Studies. His conclusions are as under:

– During the course of investigation I met a large number of people, both official and non-official, and it is my impression that, by and large, people are satisfied with the working of the *Nyaya Panchayats*. In certain quarters there has been even vehement criticism of this institution so much so that a few of the critics have gone to the extent of recommending its abolition. My own definite view, based upon close investigation, is that the *Nyaya Panchayats* do not deserve wholesale condemnation. To a large extent they have justified their existence. They have brought justice to the very doorsteps of the villagers–justice which is cheap, speedy and free from such procedural technicalities upon which the lawyer community feeds. In stead of prolonged litigations they have helped the parties considerably in reaching compromise. They have been found useful in lessening the burden of the regular courts. Generally, the people are satisfied with the judgements delivered by them. Only in about 10 per cent of their judgements, the parties have cared to go to the regular courts for review. In majority of cases the superior courts have upheld the judgements of the *Nyaya Panchayats*. It is true that the experiment has not been as big a success as people had dreamed of. But the limitations and defects from which they suffer are the limitations and defects of the Indian society as a whole. Institutions are run by individuals and individuals draw their inspirations and inhibitions from the social complex in which they live and move. Those who comdemn the *Nyaya Panchayats* alone, very often, fail to realize that political organizations at other levels also betray weaknesses and sometimes utter weaknesses in their working. Our *Zilla Parishads*, Municipalities, Corporations, State Legislatures and even judicial organizations have, to put mildly, not escaped lashing criticism. Even the Parliament and the Supreme Court have received their share of criticism. The bureaucracy too has developed its own defects and maladies. It is in this backdrop that the working of the *Nyaya Panchayats* has to be evaluated. The Indian society is passing through a transition. We have not been able as yet to completely shake off the feudal mentality and its accompanying complexes. The big land holders, casteism, social and religious taboos continue to play a significant role in the Indian society, specifically in rural areas. On the other hand, we have yet to fully develop those attitudes, outlook, behaviour pattern and objectivity which impart to the institutions–political, social and economic-health, vigour and alertness that make their working successful. In spite of the many defects of the *Nyaya Panchayats*, I am convinced that they should be retained. The more we remove their defects and limitations, the better they would serve the needs of the village people. The individuals who man the various institutions need reorientation in democratic thinking and outlook at all levels. This is a gradual and painful process but the way in which democracy has so far worked in India, in spite of drawbacks, encourages us to hope for better shape of things to come. Along with the many defects from which the average villager suffers, he has in his possession a robust common sense. He may take time to change his masters, but he is shrewd enough to realise where the shoe pinches and has shown no hesitation in throwing out those who govern him, If he finds that their continuance in office is detrimental to his interests.

- The one major defect in the working of the *Nyaya Panchayats* is that the enthusiasm for this institution is slowly diminishing and the blame for it must be put squarely on the shoulders of short lived cabinets in the state which persistently refused to hold elections of the *panchayats*. After the third election (1961-62) no election could be held until 1972. The different coalition cabinets during the period for purely political reasons, felt shy to face the electorate. This resulted in making a considerable number of *Nyaya Panchayats* defunct. The elections of the *Panchayats* must be held regularly, if they are expected to come upto the expectations of the framers of the Act.

- The first step that I would suggest towards their improvement is to organise training course for the *panchs* immediately after their elections. The course should include lectures, accompanied with the distribution of hand books written in simple and intelligible language on the aims, aspirations, powers and procedure of the *Nyaya Panchayats*. The programmes should also include moot courts. The training programmes should be organised at block headquarters. It should be made incumbent upon all the *panchs* to attend the training programme. The Sub-Divisional Magistrate/*Munsif* should be directed to attend the programme and point out the mistakes generally committed by the *Nyaya Panchayats* in the disposal of cases. I would also suggest that apart from the training programmes, annual *Panch Sammelan* at the block level should be organised as a platform for exchange of views relating to the work. They would also act as transmission belts between the *panchs* and the Government.

- Our analysis shows that the circles of the *Nyaya Panchayats* are much larger in area and have proved inconvenient both to the litigants and *panchs*. It is, therefore, suggested that the size of circle should be reduced and the area of each circle should cover not more than three or four *Gram Sabhas* even though it would mean additional expenditure for the Governments. This reform, would also satisfy the spirit of decentralisation.

- Our investigations show that the *panchs* do not regularly attend the sittings, resulting in postponement of cases and the consequent harassment to the litigants. This is also true about the *Panchayat* secretaries. Their absence from the sittings of the *Nyaya Panchayats* is responsible for frequent irregularities in their proceedings. My firm suggestion is that the Government must take necessary steps to reduce the frequency of absenteeism on the part of the *Panchs* and the *Panchayat* secretaries.

- I also suggest that for the appointment of *Panchs* the practice of reference to the Advisory Committee should be discontinued. The committees have proved unnecessary. They only delay matters. Overwhelmingly, their role has only been to endorse the names recommended by the Sub-Divisional Officers. Any member of the *gram panchayat* should be at liberty to approach the District Magistrate if he has any grievance against the recommendations of the Sub-Divisional Officers.

- Our analysis has shown that the *Nyaya Panchayats* do not possess adequate power to execute decrees or recover fines. They have no power to attach or auction property to recover the amount of decree or fines. For this the competent authority is the *munsif* in civil cases and the Sub-Divisional Magistrate in criminal cases. It is, therefore, suggested that necessary amendments should be made in the Act to empower the *Nyaya Panchayats* to issue warrants of attachment directly and the *Lekhpals* be required to act as *Kurk Amins*, too.

* Another suggestion which should be seriously considered with regard to the provision relating to the review of judgements of the *Nyaya Panchayats* is that, at present no appeal is allowed. It would be better if a two-tier system of village judiciary is established. Apart from the *Nyaya Panchayat* in each circle, there should be an appellate court also at the block level consisting of *panchs* elected by the *panchs* of the circle constituting the block. The judgements of the block level *panchs* would be subject to review by the regular courts. It would give the disputants another opportunity to be heard before going to the regular superior court. This would also add to the importance of village judiciary.

Another useful study on the working of *Nyaya Panchayats* in Uttar Pradesh was done by Mr. Richard L. Abel, School of Law, University of California, Los Angeles, entitled, "The Politics of Informal Justice". While commenting on ideological and structural dimension of *Nyaya Panchayat* operations, he says:

– Previous studies have highlighted the ideological confusion surrounding *Nyaya Panchayats* in U.P. and other parts of India. Three separate roles and associated goals have been and still are being, urged for *Nyaya Panchayat*: as an arm of the state judicial service; as branch of the Community Development Programme and lastly, a modified version of the traditional *panchayats*. As a part of the state judicial system, *Nyaya Panchayat* (separated from *panchayats* exercising administrative authority in accordance with Article 50 of the Constitution) were to displace existing indigenous institutions - whether based on caste, villages or other groupings and carry state powers and a constitutional vision of India in rural areas. Alternately, *Nyaya Panchayats* were to assist in the reformation of the rural society by providing practical experience in handling village affairs and educating the general public about their privileges and obligation in an independent India. The skills and experience of traditional village leaders were to be channelled up to new elective bodies, and *Nyaya Panchayats* were also to involve those unaccustomed into asserting themselves in local arenas. Lastly *Nyaya Panchayat* were to serve symbolically and practically as informal, accessible *panchayats* and to adopt many of the traits of traditional *panchayats* to buttress this role.

– Reports on Indian legal system and administration of justice have reiterated the government's devotion to the *panchayat* and reflect what can best be called the dominance of the "*Panchayat* Ideology". Both the National Report on Judicare and the Ashok Mehta Committee Report on *Panchayati Raj* note a decline in the current *Nyaya Panchayat* systems in U.P. and other Indian states but supported its retention and recommend smaller bodies, larger budgets and slightly enhanced jurisdiction. However, in the intervening years no state has adopted these recommendations or otherwise altered the *Nyaya Panchayat* system although some have abolished it altogether. Scholarly resistance to the notion of the failure of *Nyaya Panchayat* also supports the concept of a *panchayat* ideology, that is a belief in the efficacy of the *panchayat* in resolving disputes in rural areas in the face of strongly inconsistent evidence. This ideology is one component of rural justice in India.

– *Nyaya Panchayats* have civil jurisdiction in pecuniary claim under Rs. 500 (unless both parties agree to submit a larger amount) involving money due on contracts not affecting interests in immovable property, compensation for wrongfully taking or damaging property and recovery of movable property. Criminal jurisdiction is more extensive and covers a substantial range of offences under the I.P.C. and specialised statutes. The *Nyaya Panchayat* are authorised to levy fines upto Rs. 100 but they have no power to sentence offenders to imprisonment even for failure to pay fine.

They also have the power to admonish in some cases and can compensate the victim out of the fines collected. The state government retains the power to enhance the *Nyaya Panchayat* jurisdiction as well as diminish it if there is "admission of miscarriage of justice".

– Two essential features of lay adjudication, simplicity of procedure and flexibility of functioning, are realised in the design of *Nyaya Panchayat*. These are not encumbered by the need to follow elaborate rules of civil and criminal procedure or the law of evidence. Complaints may be made orally or in writing; no legal representation is allowed, although in some civil matters parties may be represented by an "agent". Witnesses, if any, are examined on oath or solemn affirmation. After the parties present evidence and argument informally, they are asked to absent themselves; *panchs* confer among themselves and arrive at the decision which is pronounced in open court. A judgement is written and signed by the parties. Despite these informal attributes *Nyaya Panchayats* do differ from the traditional dispute resolving institutions in several significant respects. Membership is fixed, rather than flexible and based indirectly on popular election rather than social standing. *Nyaya Panchayat* constituencies are territorial units rather than functional or ascriptive groups. They decide by majority votes rather than consensus. They are required to follow statutory law. Because they are supported by the government, they can assess minor court fees, issue summons, proceed *ex parte* in the case of a recalcitrant party, they are required to maintain records of evidence, judgements and all *panchayat* transactions and are subordinate to higher civil and criminal courts through the sub-district magistrate, their decisions can be appealed in a few limited areas.

According to Abel, several structural weaknesses are apparent in *Nyaya Panchayats* in Uttar Pradesh:

– First, the system of constituting *Nyaya Panchayats* through a combination of election and nomination helps to render the public apathetic and fearful of official favouritism and increases factionalism in local *panchayat* elections. The "indirect" method authorises the district magistrate to act on recommendations of lower officials and nominate influential persons from the *gram panchayat* to serve on *Nyaya Panchayat* benches. This can degenerate with a mechanical endorsement of untrustworthy suggestions by these officials. At the same time eligible elites compete energetically for *gram panchayat* and *Nyaya Panchayat* positions. Moreover, infrequent elections discourage public interest in the electoral process.

– Second, the limited jurisdiction powers outlined earlier reduce the effectiveness of *Nyaya Panchayat* decision. Criminal cases of theft and misuse may not involve property worth more than Rs. 50; overlapping jurisdiction allow police to send cases cognizable by a *Nyaya Panchayat* to the *Munsif* or judicial magistrate and the latter readily accept application to transfer cases from *Nyaya Panchayat*. In a particular sub-division it transpired that every *Nyaya Panchayat* decision had atleast one procedural error making every application for revision technically meritorious.

Lacking authority to send parties to jail, *Nyaya Panchayats* must rely on the police and the sub-district magistrate to enforce their orders. Of the few fines levied, most were never collected. In one particular case, several men had been found guilty of a criminal offence and fined Rs. 100 each but none was willing to comply with the judgement. They threatened the *sarpanch* and urged him to reverse the decision. After some days the *sarpanch* met the guilty men and told them confidentially that if fines were not paid, the opposing party would seek revision and drag the case into the judicial magistrate's court. Once the case was there, the *sarpanch* argued, he could not predict what would happen. Within a few days each of the men paid a fine of Rs. 99 and the *sarpanch* had no further trouble with them.

– Third, low budgets reduce *Nyaya Panchayat* activities considerably. There was no permanent meeting place nor any permanent *chaprasis* to call witnesses and serve processes. Small fees did not allow the *Nyaya Panchayat* to build a large reserve.

– Fourth, the low educational level of the *panchs* makes it difficult for them to handle the procedural technicalities of *Nyaya Panchayat* operations. The sole requirements of *panch* is that he or she be thirty years old and be able to read and write Hindi in the *Devanagiri* script. The semi-literate *panchs* expressed concern that the manuals, forms and procedures provided for *Nyaya Panchayats* were too complicated for them to understand and said that they left things to the *sarpanch* to decipher. None of the *sarpanchs* or *panchs* had ever been to the training sessions on the *Nyaya Panchayats* by district *Panchayati Raj* officials. Lack of *Panchayati Raj* funds limited the number of classes offered and *panchs* served, but most said that they could not afford to take time off from work to attend, in any case.

– Fifth, even more confusing than the rules and regulations are the conflicting roles and duties that *sarpanchs* and *panchs* are supposed to perform. They are to be honest, upright, and impartial, sensitive to the needs of the parties, responsive to the situation, energetic in reporting information and declaring rights and wrongs; fair in reaching a suitable compromise and forceful in levying and collecting a fine with hardly any means to do so. They are judges but act only as a body. By accepting nominations to the *Nyaya Panchayats*, they lose the power and prestige that goes with the membership in the *Gram Panchayats* (which administers local development programmes and is active in local politics) but confirm the power and positions they already possess as local leaders. The rules they apply are a mixture of official law and local custom which must be acceptable to a population that knows little about it. And all this is to be done without compensation.

– Only those with time, money and local support are interested in getting the positions in *Nyaya Panchayats*. These are persons with control of substantial landholdings and large political base. Due to various factors *sarpanchs* serve for years. Competition is limited to opposing village factions, often amorphous and unstable, and position of leaders depend on their success in suppressing internal opposition. Factions were already present in the villages prior to the introduction of electoral politics, these have now come to play a major role in elections. One strategy is to create alliances and bargains across previously established lines. A common result is a battle for position among a few contenders and their supporters. Most villagers do not view the *Nyaya Panchayats* as representative, or as an impartial body. Failure of *Nyaya Panchayats* in Uttar Pradesh must stem partially from the institutional structure that perpetuates traditional patterns of local dominance and offers little reasons for confidence in its decisions.

Abel's observations of *Nyaya Panchayat* in the Bharatpur region revealed that their actual operations do not correspond to the statutory requirements. Rules are followed or ignored as *sarpanch* chooses. *Nyaya Panchayats* meetings are irregular, quorums are usually not met and *panchs* and parties in *Nyaya Panchayat* meetings exhibit considerable confusion. Mostly, the procedure in cases that are filed with *Nyaya Panchayats* does not conform to statutes and rules. The emphasis in *Nyaya Panchayats* seemed to be on compromise and reconciliation. Yet behind this ideal of compromise lies the coercion power of the *sarpanch. Nyaya Panchayats* are not only inconsistent but somewhat arbitrary but also slow. Cases last a few months, even years. Caste factor, stratification and local politics militate against the use of *Nyaya Panchayats* as a forum for airing and settling disputes. For most people the forum with social utility are customary unofficial caste *panchayats*, traditional village leaders, or regular state courts. Traditional caste *panchayats*, ad hoc meetings of the *Gram Panchayats* and *charismatic lok adalats* operate in UP and elsewhere in northern India because they have combined resources, authority and leadership in ways that are more acceptable and useful to the general population.

Rajasthan

A close study of the *Panchayati Raj Institutions* including the *Nyaya Panchayats* in Rajasthan was jointly undertaken by Shri M.V. Mathur, Shri Iqbal Narain and Shri V.M. Sinha. Some of their observations are as under:

- The statutory basis for *Nyaya Panchayats* has been provided by the Rajasthan Panchayat Act 1953 and amended in 1961. The Act empowers the state government to constitute *Nyaya Panchayat* in contiguous *panchayat* circles by modification in the state gazette. Usually the number of such circles should be between five and seven. But the *Nyaya Panchayat* could be established for a lesser number of such circles also if the state government decides to do so.

- The Rajasthan Panchayat Act provides that elections will be indirect and that all members shall be elected from each of the *panchayat* areas. The actual method of elections is not provided in the Act. This has been left to the discretion of the state government. Obviously, the state government can change the manner of election any time it deems fit. The qualifications needed for elections as member of a *Nyaya Panchayat* are (i) a person must have completed 30 years of age, (ii) must be able to read and write Hindi, (iii) must not suffer from any disqualification mentioned in Section 11 of the Act, (iv) must not be a *sarpanch, panch*, a member of the *panchayat samiti*, *pradhan* of the *Panchayat Samiti*, *pramukh* of the *Zilla Parishad* or a member thereof, a member of any standing committee of the *Panchayat Samiti*, a member of the legislative assembly or of either House of Parliament.

- *Nyaya Panchayat* is elected for a period of 6 years with nearly one-third retiring every second year by rotation. No one is allowed to be a member of more than one *Nyaya Panchayat* concurrently.

- The act requires the Chairman to constitute benches. Each bench should have at least three members. The Chairman may or may not be included in any bench. State Government has the power to regulate the procedure, the number of sittings, etc. by making rules. Every member of the *Nyaya Panchayat*, the Chairman and officers of the administrative staff of the *Nyaya Panchayat* (including the secretary and peon) are public servants, within the meaning of the Indian Penal Code and are entitled to protection under the Judicial Officers Protection Act 1950 while acting as a member of a *Nyaya Panchayat*.

– *Nyaya Panchayat* enjoys both civil and criminal jurisdiction and can impose a fine upto Rs. 50 but cannot impose any other punishment. On the civil side the *Nyaya Panchayats* are competent to hear and decide cases involving amounts upto Rs. 250.

– The *Nyaya Panchayat* while discharging their duties are not bound by the Code of Criminal Procedure, Code of Civil Procedure, Indian Evidence Act, Court Fee Act and Indian Limitation Act.

– *Nyaya Panchayat* on an average serves a population of about 14 to 15 thousand people. Sometimes larger areas are recommended to augment the resources of the *Nyaya Panchayat*. However, this is not a correct approach. While there can be no two opinions about the necessity of augmenting the *Nyaya Panchayat* resources, an increase in the area of *Nyaya Panchayats* is hardly the way to do it. The area of a *Nyaya Panchayat* should be small and compact so that the villager may be afraid to tell a lie in the presence of those with whom he happens to be acquainted. If the operational areas get widened it will start functioning in the same strange atmosphere for the villager in which a court functions. Moreover it will lead to accumulation of cases.

– After the elections to *Nyaya Panchayat*, members elect a Chairman. This is done by show of hands. The Chairman constitutes the benches of the *Nyaya Panchayats*. The chances of the Chairman using his authority to constitute benches should be taken seriously. He may put himself on all benches. What is worse, the Chairman may place his favourite *nyaya panch* on several benches at the cost of other *nyaya panchs*. The *Nyaya Panchayat* does not have a large staff. Usually it has a secretary and a peon who also very often do not serve on a whole time basis. Their salaries are quite low. Further service conditions in the *Nyaya Panchayats* are really bad. Salaries are not paid regularly, a problem closely linked up with the crippled financial position of the *panchayats*. The favouritism in the appointment and of poor service conditions defeats all canons of sound personnel administration.

– Financial condition of the *Nyaya Panchayat* is critical. On an average their revenue comes to about Rs. 3,000 a year. A substantial portion of this revenue comes from the *panchayat*. The contribution from *panchayat* remains unpaid because in many cases *panchayat* themselves are not financially well off. Other sources of income of the *Nyaya Panchayat* are court fees and fines. Experience in this behalf was also not very happy. In one case only Rs. 2 were collected as against the estimated income of Rs. 500 from the fines. Such income thus does not go very far in improving the financial conditions of the *Nyaya Panchayats*.

Not only the finances of the *Nyaya Panchayat* are meagre, the process of collecting court fee is also cumbersome. It goes without saying that a drastic improvement in financial resources of the *Nyaya Panchayats* is essential for their efficiency as an organ of judicial administration.

– The establishment of the *Nyaya Panchayat* has definitely brought the seat of justice closer to the people. Justice is no longer being administered for the village folk in strange atmosphere by a magistrate who does not share most of their value judgements. It is now being administered almost right at their door by their kinsmen who are a part of the village community.

As a corollary to the above advantage, the litigants may find it difficult to indulge in any falsehood when justice is administered by their kinsmen. The whole village community has received the *Nyaya Panchayat* well. It is probable that the cases going to courts from villages have lessened.

- Furthermore, the institution of *Nyaya Panchayat* has encouraged the principle of conciliation as a way of deciding disputes. Surprisingly, conciliation is being successfully resorted to not so much at the initial stage of judgement as at the review stage. This is rather intriguing situation. At whatever stage it is used the method of conciliation for resolving village disputes is an advantage from the sociological point of view.

- However, all is not well with the working of *Nyaya Panchayats*.

  (a) In certain cases the members do not seem to take the meetings of *Nyaya Panchayat* seriously. On a number of occasions no meeting of *Nyaya Panchayat* could be held for want of quorum. The working of *Nyaya Panchayat* lacks the glamour of executive authority associated with *Panchayat Samitis* and *Panchayats*. Secondly, the *Nyaya Panchs* are not paid any allowances. This is a positive hardship since a *panch* has always to travel to some village other than his own. Travelling in the rural areas is fairly time consuming and bothersome even when members may be entitled to allowances.

  (b) It has come to notice that the *Nyaya Panchayats* take unduly long to decide cases. According to one study the time taken for the disposal of criminal cases ranges from one to fifteen months. This delay is distressing. The delay is all the more regretable when there are several benches to handle cases. One of the most important factors for the delay is the lack of interest of its members in the work of *Nyaya Panchayats*. Closely related to the issue of delay is the question of accumulation of arrears of cases in *Nyaya Panchayats*.

(c) After cases have been decided and the compliance is not forthcoming, the *Nyaya Panchayat* reopens the suit for consideration. The study shows that a very large number of cases are reopened by the *Nyaya Panchayats* by way of review. At the reconsideration stage an understanding is arrived at in most cases, failing which some penalty is imposed. It is felt that such a compromise should be brought about by the *Nyaya Panchayats* in the first instance and not at the review stage lest it becomes disadvantageous rather than useful. Furthermore, the practice of concessions at the review stage is likely to affect the reputation of the *Nyaya Panchayat* as nobody would comply with the requirements of the judgement in the hope that at the stage of reconsideration some considerations may be granted.

(d) This practice is also against the accepted canons of judicial administration which demands that the court should not reconsider its own decision except for the correction of minor clerical errors. It is necessary that both in order to maintain decorum and in the interests of justice that once a judgement is delivered the chapter should be closed as far as the *Nyaya Panchayat* is concerned. When the parties refuse to comply with its decision, *Nyaya Panchayat* should refer the matter to the Sub Divisional Officer asking him to realise the fines as if it was imposed by him.

(e) Closely related is the problem of executing *Nyaya Panchayat* decisions. The *Nyaya Panchayats* have to depend on Sub Divisional Officer or some other subordinate executive machinery for the execution of their decisions. Very often adequate cooperation is not available from these agencies. It is feared that since *Nyaya Panchayat* decisions are likely to take very long for execution people may prefer to take the cases to the courts where they are hopeful for early execution. A maximum time limit of a fortnight or three weeks for execution, of *Nyaya Panchayat* orders may be prescribed through the rules by the government.

In conclusion, the team led by Shri M.V. Mathur, Shri Iqbal Narain and Shri V.M. Sinha, stated that, the constitution of *Nyaya Panchayats* is today the least controversial of the *Panchayati Raj Institutions*. It is perhaps one of those institutions which commands both prestige and confidence of the villagers. Its defects and shortcomings are largely administrative and procedural and as such within the orbit of administrative improvement. Efforts should be made to see that the administration of *Nyaya Panchayat* both financial and procedural is streamlined soon, so that the institution gains in internal strength to sustain the confidence that the villagers have reposed in the institution. Extra care should be taken to ensure that politics for power which has already started vitiating other *Panchayati Raj Institutions* does not affect *Nyaya Panchayats*. It is in this context that it is a happy step that judicial functions were taken away from the *panchayats* and entrusted to separate institutions, i.e. *Nyaya Panchayats*. Previously when judicial and executive functions were combined in the *panchayats* the chances of politics of power corrupting the judicial process were far greater than what they are today when there exist *Nyaya Panchayats* as separate custodians of justice.

Karnataka

Owing to the serious efforts of Sri Ramakrishna Hegde and Nazir Sab very comprehensive and far reaching innovations were made through an enactment relating to *Panchayati Raj Institutions*. Dr. Upendra Baxi, an eminent jurist, made a detailed analysis in an address entitled, "Participatory Justice: A Critique of *Nyaya Panchayats*". I reproduce below Dr. Upendra Baxi's observations *in toto*.

At the outset, permit me to raise a question as to whether decentralisation is really a direct problem of the people. I do not believe that it is. To my mind it is a problem of the managers of the people. Managers of the people have a large number of problems and they try to solve them in one way or the other. India is the only country perhaps where a mistake is made all along in thinking that solving the problems of the managers of the people really is solving the problems of people themselves.

Of course, that does not happen even though our land is a land of miracles.

There are a set of problems like role of governors, distribution of powers, presidential or prime ministerial form of government, decentralisation and so on. Are these problems really the problems of the Indian masses. The social and economic proletariat of India or the *Atisudras*, as Ambedkar called them, remains untouched by the *herapheri* of those in power who influence the distribution and management of powers.

I have come for this seminar out of a special affection for very worthwhile experiment that has been launched by Ramakrishna Hegde, Nazir Sab and others in Karnataka. Certainly, it is a very far-reaching innovation, if implemented. There is always this if; IF's of implementation are vetoes on objectives of policies in India. But I am sure there is sufficient amount of political will, at least there is sufficient political imagination to devise a new form of decentralisation in Karnataka. It is an excellent beginning. It represents an advancement on the thinking of decentralisation.

Colonial Model of Law Making

When the bill was being drafted I had an occasion to see it and also to remark that a Bill which goes into 319 Articles or Sections (I am not counting the sub-sections, explanations and proviso), and the Bill which like the Constitution of India has five Schedules (whereas our Constitution has nine), is itself an enemy of decentralisation in any genuine sense. After all when law is made, it is for the people to operate on the ground level–*mandal panchayats, gram sabha* and so on. We need an absolutely new legislative approach where the legal language of drafting which would invariably be exploited by dominant classes for their own ends, should be minimized. I think it is possible to write briefer and simpler laws which can communicate and help people.

The Bill follows the colonial method of drafting legislation where we find words upon words and the weight of the words is supposed to represent a dynamic social change. I do not see the political imagination extended here to a new way of designing law which will communicate to the people without the help of intermediaries.

Dissolution Provision

I am also sorry to note (and in saying this I do not detract from the warmth of my appreciation of Ramakrishna Hegde's efforts) that this Act, like all *Panchayat* Acts, provides for the dissolution of *Panchayats* by the Government. Therefore, it robs of its radical fervour of its objectives by the continuation of this form of power. I remember Ramakrishna Hegde held a very important seminar on Centre-State relations in Bangalore a couple of years ago. It was a star-studded seminar of the national intelligentia and they were discussing all kinds of issues following which a mammoth report has now come out. I distinctly remember the Chief Minister's speech in which he said that Article 356, which authorise the imposition of President's rule over the states should be removed. There is a multi-party consensus demanding the deletion of Article 356. The issue is before the Sarkaria Commission.

The point I am making is, that I am not in disagreement with the demand to remove Articles 356 in part, I strongly support it for very good reasons. But then, that very party comes to write a document on *Panchayat*, it provides for the same kind of contradiction–local bodies, grass root bodies can be dissolved by the state. Undoubtedly, the Karnataka Act inches forward by providing that *Parishads* and *Mandals* may not be dissolved by a stroke of a pen without any rational explanation and opportunity to be heard. It also provides for re-elections within six months of dissolution.

So there are, some safeguards of natural justice provided. But the power of dissolution also remains like a Damocles sword. Section 271 must be recast to discipline the power of the Government to dissolve these bodies by specifying exceptional circumstances for such drastic action.

Section 271 providing for dissolution is far too wide. It provides six situations in which a *Zilla Parishad* can dissolve *Mandal Panchayats* including its "incompetence". The Government can similarly dissolve a *Zilla Parishad* on five grounds including its "incompetence". Surely, "incompetence", for example, is no ground on which Article 356 power can be exercised by the President. Default in performance of duties imposed by law is another ground for dissolution. Surely, grassroot bodies must not be in such defaults; but should that be ground for their dissolution? Most state governments, and even the Union of India, chronically default on their statutory duties; but surely, there are other ways than dissolution which can rectify such defaults. The powers for dissolution are just too wide.

One does not look at this Bill only as a Bill of a particular government but it is a law that will outlast or see many changes in the power structure in Karnataka, in the next thirty to fifty years, ensuring institutionalized dignity to these bodies. These bodies should not be subjected to overweening uncanalised executive power. This is my general observation.

As I said, the Bill is an exemplary piece of legislation in the neo-colonial model of drafting laws. It is tolerably clear, it is long and complex in certain aspects but I suppose that is inherent in the model of law-making that we adopted.

Decentralisation

This brings me to my major dispute on the whole notion of decentralisation versus participation. I think managers of the people all over the world are concerned with reproduction of state power in all their attempts; reproduction of ruling ideologies, proliferation of those ideologies to the grassroots level. If decentralisation is really managerial problem, it involves transfer or delegation of power. It is based necessarily on a top-down perspective, not what is called the bottom-up perspective of distribution of power. This was exactly what the British wanted to give us; a dominion status with certain devolution of powers (not independence) and we rejected it. We have rejected it only to replicate it within the framework of an independent India.

We opposed the devolution idea as a bad idea because it was inimical to *Swaraj* or freedom. Gandhiji's concept was very rich. He said *Swaraj* would begin after *Swaraj* was achieved. If that notion of *Swaraj* still pervades us, obviously there should be an emphasis on participatory grassroots democracy. While the Karnataka legislation is a significant beginning in that direction, the overall scheme is one where there is no real sharing of power. Which is to say that at the participatory level, it is merely a delegation or transfer or devolution of power. One must take the political realities of any legislative exercise into account when one talks about legislations. I am doing nothing more than that. Perhaps it is not possible for any government in India to attempt no matter how accepted the government is, how strong the majority is, how good the leaders are, to move away from a colonial method of governance–a colonial method of distribution of power and a colonial or neo-colonial method of management of distribution of power. If we are locked into it then decentralization is obviously the only strategy available. I wonder, however, why should we be locked in it.

The law is again bound in a traditional circuit of governance which really treats people as subject rather than citizens there is, of course, a great distinction to be made between the category of subjects and category of citizens. The real notion of *Panchayati Raj* in the model of decentralisation of power is locked up into three or four typical images of what *Panchayati Raj* could be. None of these images has anything to do with real sharing of power by people with the elected representatives of the people, or the managers of the people.

For example, *panchayats* can be, broadly speaking, looked upon as political agencies. *Panchayati Raj Institutions* are designed towards the reproduction of the power of certain political formations, parties and their ideologies. *Panchayati Raj* secures mobilisation of people or leaders or local leaders of the people; not the people themselves. This is one way of looking at what constitutes the political perspective of *Panchayati Raj institutions* and that has been one dominant objective of *Panchayati Raj institutions.*

The other dominant image or objective of *Panchayati Raj institutions* in my understanding of it, right from the Balwantrai Mehta Committee Report to the present legislation, has been the progressive extension of administrative state power. That is, you worry about local self-government, you worry about transfer of petty decision-making at petty levels, while simultaneously safeguarding the real position of interests and power at higher levels of centralisation.

The third image of *Panchayati Raj institutions* in India has been one of these being developmental agencies. This is predominant, and it is welcome, in the Karnataka legislation. It is one of the most explicit legislations which regards *Panchayati Raj institutions* as development agencies. Of course, the mechanism here is not sharing of power as such, but the delegation of power and transfer of functions.

Finally, without being exhaustive, there is the Gandhian perspective which regards *Panchayati Raj institutions* quite differently in terms of a kind of revivalistic movement for restoring communitarian institutions to the countryside. The Gandhian perception of *Panchayati Raj* shudders at the political, administrative, or developmental approach.

Broadly speaking, it seems to me that the Karnataka legislation is locked into the national circuit which thinks of *Panchayati Raj institutions* either as developmental or administrative or as marginally political mechanisms. This is something to be noted and does not imply any criticism.

The Karnataka legislation does, to my pleasant surprise, take into account certain new tasks that *Mandal Panchayats* have to perform like solicitude for the weaker sections of the society, scheduled castes, scheduled tribes, and so on. But like all *panchayati* thinking in the decentralization model, it has to overlook and cannot cater to very many vital areas. For example, it overlooks whole areas of atrocities on untouchables and tribals and women; agrestic serfdom; bonded labour or slavery or the whole area of abuse of power at micro-levels repressing activists or change-agents trying to implement what the law says or the Constitution says–thus enabling the *Gram Sabha*, the *Mandal Panchayat* and *Zilla Parishad* to become significant actors in these areas of exploitation, inequality and injustice. Why should they not be an integral part of the agenda of *panchayati raj* organization is a question which arises only from a perspective which refuses to regard decentralisation as the only objective of *Panchayati Raj institutions*. If the idea of *Panchayati Raj* is only to decentralise and delegate, obviously these are not the areas that would go to *Panchayati Raj institutions*, they are high-tension areas; high visibility areas of human rights which are highly susceptible to delegitimation, partisan governments and obviously they are not delegated to local bodies.

Nyaya Panchayats

There seems to be tendency to avoid national level courts from getting into problems that are small, petty, localised. Again the idea is not to democratise judicial administration through *Nyaya Panchayats* anywhere. The idea is not to promote greater access to justice. The idea is to unblock the arteries of major institutions of judiciary. Therefore, what remains for the *Nyaya Panchayats* is marginal jurisdiction which is of no major significance for the people themselves although it does lighten some of the burdens of the District Court, High Court and the Supreme Court. It is a kind of siphon process. There is, therefore, limited jurisdiction.

I am happy to see that the Karnataka Bill is very generous in its Schedule 3 and it includes substantial criminal jurisdiction including voluntarily causing hurt, a sort of use of criminal force. I suppose that this will be properly interpreted and handled, including in its purview atrocities against the weaker sections of the community, exploitation of labour, practice of untouchability, and so on. But I would have been happier if the *Nyaya Panchayats* were given exclusive powers in regard to enforcement of the Protection of Civil Rights Act 1976 because untouchability is essentially practiced in the rural areas. It would have been better if certain forms of offences, where the permission of the state government is to be taken under the Prevention of Corruption Act, could also have been transferred here because local abuses of power are the real problem of the people in the countryside. Since some new extension of criminal jurisdiction is already made in *Nyaya Panchayat*, one feels that more should have been there. But for the Karnataka Legislation, I do not think one would have expected or made a demand for including the serious criminal offences which are now included. But I do hope that the Schedule 3, so far as criminal legislation is concerned, is expanded further.

Otherwise, of course, the Karnataka Legislation follows the national pattern in giving marginal importance to the *Nyaya Panchayats*. There is a very interesting list under sub-section (b). Offences under a lot of Acts, which include not only the Cattle Trespass Act but also include a large number of Vaccination Acts. The Vaccination Act of 1950, the Hyderabad Vaccination Act of 1951, the Central Act of 1880 (I do not know what kind of vaccination was available in 1880) and the Prevention of Cruelty to Animals Act. I am sure there are a large number of equally important laws such as vaccination laws which could be given for the administration to *Nyaya Panchayat*. Interestingly, the Vaccination Acts are coupled with the Primary Education Act. I do not know what the two have to do with each other, but it seems to me that they have been listed rather randomly. Again I would say that this is not a shortcoming in the Karnataka approach, it is our national heritage. We do not know how to decentralise judicial administration. We are, unfortunately, confusing hierarchy with wisdom and hierarchy with ability all the time; that is the Hindu view of life. We think a *munsif* or a District judge or a High Court judge is somehow a better judge than the lay persons in the villages. Therefore, I must say that the organisation of *Nyaya Panchayats* is slightly infected by the national virus or the national confusion over decentralisation of judicial remedies.

The *Nyaya Panchayat* will be coming into being after five years. That means Karnataka has some more time. May I offer some non-development wisdom on the issue of *Nyaya*

Panchayat? I hope that whenever the states implement it, the jurisdiction could be revised without making it an aggressive institution which will go and attack all the evils at the local level, without disarming the institution from doing what matters to people at the grassroots. The *munsif* courts, the district court or high courts are simply not accessible to masses of people, and therefore, one may begin to think that *Nyaya Panchayat* could make a very serious alternate beginning in the indigenisation of judicial administration in India. In fact, through Karnataka's efforts, one can cultivate national level opinion. Now the Law Reform Commission is headed by Justice Desai, formerly of the Supreme Court, who has always said that our system of justice is Anglo-Saxon and the administration tends it here and there to get the results it wants. Now that the Prime Minister has made a very astute move by putting Justice Desai as the Chairman of the Law Commission of India, he is in a difficult situation of having to live up all his judicial rhetoric. But I am sure if there is one man who will try to live up to it, it is Justice Desai and, therefore, one may persuade him to examine the whole question, that is the first term of reference of the Law Commission, viz. reforms of the administration of Justice. This is nothing new. Each Law Commission has been given this task. Each Law Commission interprets reform to mean the mere administration of justice, more judges on the High Court, more benches of the High Courts, more salary for High Courts, and how to deal with the problems of arrears after having created them in the first place.

This is a tradition. But one should hope for some change in the thinking of the Law Commission and therefore of the Government of India in the sphere of democratisation of judicial administration. So far, wherever the *Nyaya Panchayats* have functioned they have functioned essentially as the assaulting arm of state power on local institutions. They have tended to displace the existing fora which are traditional. They are not always just, and by the same token all that is modern is also not just. They displace traditional forms of dispute settlement like the *Baradari Panchayat*, the caste *panchayat* or *panchayat* dispute settlement procedures developed by social agencies, voluntary agencies, social activists in certain areas. The Indian state never meant to do justice to the *Nyaya Panchayats* because it did not want them to be active, and it did this by the application of principles of liberal jurisprudence. For example, in Rajasthan, Maharashtra and elsewhere (it is true of Karnataka also) the idea is that the *Nyaya Panchayats* should be impartial. The *Nyaya Panchayats* should, therefore, not come from the same village, where a dispute has arisen. So a *Nyaya Panchayat* from an adjoining village will come to the village. Now the idea of impartiality is secured. But of course, the idea of efficiency is lost because there is much regard for a man trying to settle disputes in a village who does not know the problems of the village. Dispute settlement is an extremely sensitive matter and all anthropological accounts suggest that in village dispute settlements, the elders often meet to settle a particular dispute and, at the end, they settle disputes that lie behind this dispute, going back to generations.

So the disputing behaviour there is entirely of a different order and, therefore, this application of the notion of impartially really means that whatever little status and authority and efficiency, *Nyaya Panchayat* has failed. In Maharashtra and Rajasthan it has now been accepted that it is not worth maintaining such impartiality. Therefore, the solution is to abandon *Nyaya Panchayats*. We can be more loyal than the English to liberal principles of jurisprudence. Therefore, these are some of the problems I hope Karnataka will consider in the coming four or five years. I hope implementation of *Nyaya Panchayat* will be done before five years.

I would, at the end, suggest that the Constitution has now fortunately been amended by the much discussed and tainted amendment called the 42nd Amendment of the Constitution. That Constitutional Amendment has brought in several ideas –that we are a socialist constitution and we have fundamental duties, etc. but relevant to our discussion would be Article 39 (a) in the Directive Principles of State Policy. Article 39(a) is a wonderful article. It says that the legal system shall be so organised as to provide justice. This means from 1950 to 1976 it was not so organised. Otherwise the Constitution did not have to state this in 1976. I am a lawyer and I tend to take these words very seriously. Just as the chapter on fundamental duties says it shall be the duty of every citizen to cherish the noble ideas of the struggle of independence. Any way 39 (a) is very important. It is a charter for reorganising the legal system and it also says that it should be re-organised through schemes which provide for removal of economic and other disabilities in access to justice. We all understand economic difficulties and if we do not we have Prof. Lakdawala to explain them to us. But what are those other disparities that the Constitution talks about?

I think the other difficulties that prevent access to justice is the organisation of administration of justice itself in India. The Constitution does not say it in so many words; but that is the other disability. The main disability in access to justice is the administration of the judicial system so far as masses of Indian people are concerned and even classes of India are concerned. Therefore, the point in relation to *Nyaya Panchayat* is that the only way you can provide access to justice to rural India is by restoring the process known to India for thousands of years; that is the process of participatory justice where self-determination exists in doing of justice by the people concerned. In the tradition of intervention by elders (whether it is secular elders or *Gram Panchayats* or *baradaris*, or whatever), there is an immense variety and wealth right before us.

For models of participatory justice you can take the *Nagas*, *Bhils*, *Raj Gonds* or the entire tribal group in India. They have very sophisticated methods of determining the most complex disputes, as complex as those which come to the Supreme Court. These tribal tradition *panchayats* have very complex issues coming up for deliberation and decision. They are thoroughly deinstitutionalised. They do not have the power to hang any one. They do not have the power to send anyone to jail. They do not have the power of the kind that the state law has. Nevertheless they have a whole variety of sanctions and sanctioning mechanisms which have worked for centuries. I am not being a revivalist in that sense. I am talking as a person who has tried to study these processes which I call non-state law; which is distinct from State law in India. I am convinced that our people have not merely such a tradition but a great deal of judicial talent–talent for justice and social arrangement which we as brown English persons have decided to ignore. It is something we cannot understand. It seems to me, therefore, that the entire notion of *Nyaya Panchayats* has to cease to be a mechanism for decentralisation and delegation of judicial power and has to become an instrument of organising the tradition and talent of Indian people for doing justice.

I personally feel we need to take a total view in a dramatic experiment in popular tribunals. It can be devised in a variety of ways. There are examples of this in Sri Lanka and in Cuba where societies are at the same stages of development as in India. In India, judges are now trying fancy adventures called *Lok Adalat*–the people's court. What is this people's court? The whole idea has come from the indigenous tradition, but has been totally vulgarised by judges and lawyers. It is made in the sense of retaining or augmenting the credibility of a system which is breaking down. Now, judges come and say they are doing justice, outside the court. To my mind, it is a very significant thing because it means that courts are not able to do it during the court hours. There are a number of examples actually operating in India. I do not want to dramatise this. I am aware of miscarriages of justice. But where the local tribunals or people's tribunals are concerned, they are operative simply because the State law cannot reach there. So we at least make a fresh start in thinking in that direction.

In conclusion, I will draw a very strong distinction between the *dramatis personae* and script. The *dramatis personae* are honest; the nation should be grateful to them. One knows them as individuals and one knows what a tremendous amount of commitment and dedication they have. But unfortunately, for everybody the script is written by forces of history. We salute the political heroism of Karnataka legislators, who are the *dramatis personae*. But as we have seen, the script they articulate is composed by history, of political power in India. Let us hope that the way the script is articulated and intoned will itself influence, in the future, the very nature of political forces in India.

The Karnataka Panchayat Act of 1983 was repealed before it could be fully implemented. It was substituted by a new legislation due to political developments in the state. Shri K.S. Krishnaswamy wrote an article in the *Economic and Political Weekly* (May 1, 1993) entitled, "Karnataka's New Step Backwards". In this article, Shri Krishnaswamy has brought out that the new enactment "reveals not so much a commitment to progressive decentralisation as a unanimity among legislative members of all parties to strengthen their hold on *Panchayati Raj institutions*." I put forward his observations.

M. Y. Ghorpade, the Karnataka Minister for Rural Development and *Panchayati Raj,* has these days the air of a person who has fulfilled a mission. He has succeeded in replacing the Karnataka Zilla Parishad, Taluk Panchayat Samithis, Mandal Panchayats and Nyaya Panchayat Act of 1983, by a new Karnataka Panchayati Raj Act of 1993, as required under the Constitution (72nd Amendment) Bill 1991 which has now been ratified by a sufficient number of state legislatures to become an effective Act. His efforts have, further, been symbolically applauded by the Congress Working Committee as a model for the states; and a special session of AICC(I) is to be held at the end of May to discuss this further. No wonder Ghorpade is pleased as *panch* with what he honestly believes to be a major step forward towards decentralised government.

Purely as a matter of political upmanship, there is little doubt that Ghorpade and Moily, the Chief Minister, have won this round. Since his short tenure at the same ministry under Veerendra Patil three years back, Ghorpade had been wanting to improve upon the late Abdul Nazir Sab's original statute on decentralised governance in Karnataka. The local government structure created under that statute was a remarkable experiment in devolving political and administrative authority to *Zilla Parishads* and *Mandal Panchayats*. Undoubtedly, there was plenty of room for further advance in that direction. But the 1983 Act had a clarity of purpose, viz. "promoting the development of democratic institutions and securing a greater measure of participation by the people in the said plans and in local and governmental affairs". With this object in view, its structure and details were built around three basic principles of democracy–(i) that sovereignty vests ultimately with the people who elect the government, (ii) that those elected representatives who constitute the government of the day are accountable to people, and (iii) that no outside functionary, elected or otherwise, has any authority in the area assigned under the Constitution or statutes in force to the "local government". In the 1983 Act, only some of the developmental functions had been devolved to *Zilla Parishads* and *Mandal Panchayats*; but the promise existed of progressive transference of the full responsibility of governance–the legislative, executive and judicial functions as applicable to the area under their jurisdiction–to the *Panchayati Raj institutions*.

But Ghorpade's new bill marks no advance in any of these respects. Its purpose has in fact been quite different from the very start; and that purpose consisted of ensuring proper control over the functioning of *Zilla Parishads* and other *Panchayati Raj institutions*. Several of the new regulations in the bill are justified by him as necessary for preventing misuse and misappropriation of funds by individuals elected to office in these local bodies. In addition to tightening the control measures for these purposes, the new bill converts the two-tier system of *Zilla Parishads* and *Mandal Panchayats* in the 1983 Act into a three-tier set of *Panchayati Raj institutions* at the district, taluk and village levels as envisaged in the Constitution (72nd Amendment) Act of this year. The area of operation of the local bodies remains limited as before, to development schemes and programmes. All other governmental functions remain with the state government, which will now operate much more openly through its civil servants as a monitoring authority.

When more than two years ago, the late B. Basavalingappa and Ghorpade as ministers in-charge of *Panchayati Raj* in Veerendra Patil Government decided to modify the 1983 Act drastically, they at least had thrown open the subject for general discussion. But this time Ghorpade held everything close to his chest and revealed the full measures of his 'reforms' only at the stage of introducing the bill in the Karnataka Legislative Assembly at its last session. With its absolute majority in the assembly, the Congress government had no difficulty in securing the passage of the bill. But the Congress Party does not enjoy such control of the Legislative Council, where the combined opposition could have defeated the amendment. When things appeared as if the bill would be voted down, the Chief Minister and his minister for *Panchayati Raj* got the leaders of the opposition to a special breakfast meeting at which a deal was struck. The deal was that if the opposition helped the ruling party and passed the amending bill now, the Congress Party assured that it would incorporate later on any amendment to the new legislation which would strengthen the process of decentralisation. This assurance, according to the leader of the Janata Dal in the council who is also the leader of the opposition, had been given by the Chief Minister in the presence of some of his other colleagues and the leaders of other opposition parties.

This entire episode reveals in essence not so much a commitment to progressive decentralisation as a unanimity amongst legislative members of all parties to strengthen their hold on sub-state organisations. It is astonishing that the leaders of the Janata Dal in the two houses of the Karnataka Legislature have become a party to the new bill on nothing more than an assurance given by the Chief Minister and his colleagues at a private conclave over breakfast. If the government intended seriously to fulfill its assurance, such a private understanding should have been formalised by a full statement by the minister in the legislature, specifying the particular amendments to the new legislation which the government had undertaken to carry out after the passage of the bill. There is so far no press report of such a statement by the minister, let alone a press release by the ministry to inform the public. A major adjustment in the political structure within the state is not just a matter for the legislators to arrange as convenient to them; it is *par excellence* a matter for public discussion and electoral decision. By treating a matter of such vital importance to the people as something to be settled in a mutually advantageous manner over a cup of tea is worthy neither of the chief minister nor, especially, of the leader of the opposition. It is probably a good business-like way of doing things; but it certainly is not democracy.

Equally worrying are the implications of the new bill. By enlarging the role of the *Panchayat* at the taluk level, and by making the MLA from that constituency the chairman of that *Panchayat*, it has destroyed one of the main purpose of the earlier Act–namely, to enable the local electorate to identify government with the *Zilla Parishads* and the *Mandal Panchayats*. Similarly, in the name of ensuring proper control over *Village Panchayats*, local bodies at the taluk and district levels have been assigned monitoring powers over *Village Panchayats*, which often tense to be exercised by civil servants in the name of the governments they serve. The chief secretary of the *Zilla Parishad* and the deputy commissioner are now required to report directly to the state government. While in the case of the deputy commissioner this has always been the case, the 1983 Act had taken care to ensure (a) that the chief secretary was accountable to the *Zilla Parishad* and (b) that he would be senior to rank to the deputy commissioner, so that it would be possible for him to obtain any reports he required directly from the deputy commissioner.

The new bill changes all of this. By reinstating the MLA at the taluk level and giving him greater authority over *Village Panchayats*, the principle that *Village Panchayats* are accountable to the local electorate and not anybody else, is diluted if not totally lost. Secondly, by enlarging the role of MLAs in local bodies at all levels, it reduces the importance of the *Zilla Parishad* '*adhyakshas*' and other elected functionaries. By changing the status and responsibilities of the chief secretary, the new bill obscures the clarity that should exist between local government officers and state government officers. This has been a considerable problem since the start of the *Panchayati Raj* system in 1987; but instead of going further in the direction originally indicated–namely, converting after a period deputation of staff from state cadres to local authorities to increasing the scope for direct appointment of their officers and other staff by local bodies–the present bill is retrograde. With the passage of the new bill, a basic principle that is important in any federal structure, namely, that a person elected to the legislature of government at one tier cannot at the same time, and on the basis of the same election, be a full member of another elective body, is completely lost. The objective that the new bill fully achieves on the other hand, is to restore completely the power and the patronage of the MLAs in their constituencies, which they have all along felt, is threatened by the growth of *Panchayati Raj institutions*. Ghorpade and the leaders of the opposition parties in the Karnataka legislature have thus achieved a common objective for themselves and their members; the new bill in no way diminishes their authority through decentralised government, notwithstanding whatever Ghorpade says or assures.

Indeed it is highly questionable if the intent of the 72nd Amendment is really the creation of a decentralised polity in India. That Amendment which differed from the late Rajiv Gandhi's infructuous 64th Amendment only cosmetically, is more likely to become an instrument of strengthening the power of the central ministries at the local level via the rules and regulations that apply to development activities. It is not accidental that in the 1993-94 Budget, the largest increase in the transfer of resources from the centre to the state plans is under centrally sponsored schemes. The argument used by the centre in defence of this is precisely the same that Ghorpade uses in the case of the local governments, that is to say, to prevent misuse and misappropriation by certain individuals at the state level. When one puts all these together, it is not accidental that the Congress Working Committee should consider the latest Karnataka bill as a model to be recommended to the other states. And it is symbolic that the full-dress convention on this march towards decentralisation should be held at Amethi next month.

There is perhaps a covert purpose also. The Karnataka government is under Supreme Court orders to hold *Panchayati Raj* elections before the end of June 1993, and nothing has so far been done to fulfil that obligation. Apparently, the breakfast assurance of Moily's government has been given under duress; it badly needs fig-leaf to avoid being hauled up for contempt of court when it appears before the Supreme Court next June. Is the new bill, then, basically that fig-leaf?

I consider at this juncture, to be expedient to draw some general conclusions about the functioning of *Nyaya Panchayat*s based upon the field studies made in the states of Uttar Pradesh, Rajasthan and Karnataka.

- Generally speaking the *Nyaya Panchayats* have done some good work but their potential has not been fully exploited.

- Mostly *Nyaya Panchayats* were formed through a system of nomination or a combination of election with nomination.

- The nomination by District Magistrate who would act on the recommendation of lower functionaries would lead to influential persons being nominated to serve on *Nyaya Panchayats*. This degenerated into a mechanical endorsement of untrustworthy suggestions by the officials.

- There was a preference in some quarters for the *Nyaya Panchayat*s presided over by either retired judicial officers or members of a new service of judicial officers to be specially constituted for the purpose.

- The working of *Nyaya Panchayats* suffered because the lay members were subjected to influences and pressures.

- The working of *Nyaya Panchayats* would have improved if the lay members had received some training relating to their functions.

- The system of constituting *Nyaya Panchayat* through a combination of election and nomination helps to render the public apathetic and fearful of official favouritism and increases factionalism in local *panchayat* elections.

- Infrequent elections diminish public interest in the electoral process.

- The limited jurisdictional powers conferred on the *Nyaya Panchayats* reduced the effectiveness of their functioning.

- *Nyaya Panchayats* did not have effective wherewithal to implement their decisions. In cases of punishment of fines imposed by the *Nyaya Panchayat*s, the fines were either not realised or realised with considerable delay.

- The low educational level of the *panchs* made it difficult for them to handle the procedural technicalities of *Nyaya Panchayat* operations. This highlighted the desirability of adequate training of the *panchs*.

- Sometimes the manuals, forms and procedures prescribed for the *Nyaya Panchayats* were far too complicated for even the literate member to comprehend.

- The meetings of *Nyaya Panchayat*s were held at irregular intervals and sometimes there were inordinate delays in the disposal of cases. These delays were very injurious since they made the litigants think that *Nyaya Panchayats* functioned in the same manner as the normal judicial system.

- The attendance of *panchs* was also irregular. Some of them had to leave their own work and travel long distance. They get no compensation for loss of income. If the workload was heavy, there were bound to be serious delay in disposal due to absence of quorum in the *Nyaya Panchayat.*

- The absence of adequate finances and infrastructural facilities obstructed *Nyaya Panchayat* work.

- Caste, factions, stratification and local politics created difficulties that militated against the *Nyaya Panchayat* as a forum for settling disputes.

- Although the *Nyaya Panchayats* were constituted on the authority of statutes in various states, they (*Nyaya Panchayat*) did not receive all the support that they deserved from either the political authority or the bureaucracy. Barring a few exceptions no political party was willing to shed power to make the decentralisation a success.

– Wherever *Nyaya Panchayats* have not taken roots or wherever they have been uprooted after a brief spell of success, it was observed that the MPs and MLAs were not too friendly to these institutions and even hostile at times.

The studies relating to Uttar Pradesh, Rajasthan and Karnataka serve as a window to the situation that obtained by and large in other states. Comprehensive and critical field studies have also been conducted in respect of several other states amongst which West Bengal, Kerala, Orissa and Gujarat are worthy to mention. The most important factor that emerges out of these studies is that the political will and political awareness of the people are crucial for making the process of democratic decentralisation including the institution of *Nyaya Panchayats* successful.

Chapter 5

Framework of a Model Nyaya Panchayat

THE success of any institution largely depends on the human material that is employed to manage it. It is more so in the case of a *Nyaya Panchayat* where character, sound mental equipment and commitment are of the greatest importance to achieve the objectives enshrined in the concept of decentralization of the administration of justice.

Qualifications

On the subject of educational and other qualifications of the members of the *Nyaya Panchayats*, diverse views have been expressed. One view is that members of the *Nyaya Panchayats* should have a graduate degree as the qualification, failing which those who have gained higher secondary school examination certificate should be eligible for appointment as *Panchs*. According to this view it is sound educational background alone which would help the *Panchs* to successfully wade through the intricacies of legal work of a *Nyaya Panchayat*. There are others who believe that ability to read and write fluently and sound commonsense would be sufficient for *Panchs* to perform their functions. Still others would like to place greater emphasis on information levels as against educational levels.

It is felt that the prescription of a formal degree qualification for appointment as a member of the *Nyaya Panchayat* would deprive vast masses of people from any sense of participation in the administration of justice and indeed make the *Nyaya Panchayat* itself an elitist institution. Further, because only people from higher strata of society have access to higher education, the appointment of graduates and degree holders would in effect legitimise and perpetuate the monopoly of dominant sections of society in the administration of justice.

The administration of justice requires that the persons involved should have integrity, character, objectivity, maturity and enjoy acceptability of all sections of the community. These qualities are not necessarily brought about by a formal educational system. Nevertheless, some amount of education among members of the *Nyaya Panchayats* is indispensable. Each *Nyaya Panchayat* should have members who are able to read and write the regional language fairly and fluently. Some relaxation in this regard may have to be made in respect of *Nyaya Panchayats* in the backward and particularly tribal areas.

It is important that the *Panchs* should have adequate independent means of livelihood and be free from debt and other financial obligations. With impecuniousness, debt and other obligations, the *Panchs* cannot be expected to perform their functions in a fair and objective manner. I am not inclined to hold the view that the *Panchs* should be drawn only from the comparatively well to do sections of the society. Such an approach would go against the very democratic ideals. What we are looking for is not financial status, but character, integrity, commitment and economic independence. The presence of rich landlords may create imbalances and tension and militate against harmonious functioning of the *Nyaya Panchayats*. In a free and fair election some well to do villagers or landlords may be elected to the *Panchayats/Nyaya Panchayats*, but it would be impolitic to lay down a condition that *Panchs* should come from well to do sections of society alone.

While addressing ourselves to the question of age qualification for the *Panchs*, we have to bear in mind several important considerations. Elderly people command greater respect and following because of their maturity, experience, knowledge of local customs and traditions. In my view, the age eligibility qualification should start from forty. I am not in agreement with the view that there should not be any upper limit in respect of age. In fact, there should be a provision for the retirement of members of the *Nyaya Panchayats*. A compelling reason is that very old members of the village community, who are isolated from current realities of life and changing social mores, apart from physical incapacity and mental sterility should not be eligible for membership of the *Nyaya Panchayats*. Taking all these factors into consideration, persons eligible for election to *Nyaya Panchayats* should preferably be in the age group 40-70 years.

According to the recent Constitutional Amendments, no less than one-third of the total membership of the *Panchayati Raj institutions* has been reserved for women. This representation should be scrupulously observed while constituting the *Nyaya Panchayats*. Our Constitution does not brook any distinction on the basis of sex in matters relating to contesting for political offices or employment. Even keeping the social conditions in view, it would be extremely desirable to associate women in the trial of cases by the *Nyaya Panchayats*. If the normal process of election does not throw up women candidates to the extent of one-third of the strength of the *Nyaya Panchayats*, the requisite number should be co-opted from the village/villages concerned.

As a democratic institution, the *Nyaya Panchayat* is not expected to have any denominational bias. Its doors should be open to members of every religion, community and caste group. For the upliftment of the weaker sections of society the recent Constitutional Amendment provides reservation of seats for SC/ST candidates in proportion to the population at each level of *Panchayati Raj institutions*. Here again if the normal process of election does not bring up adequate number of SC/ST candidates the shortage may be made up by co-opting candidates drawn from village/villages concerned to serve on the *Nyaya Panchayats*.

Remuneration

At present, members of the *Nyaya Panchayat* do not get any remuneration for their services. It is my view also that a salary or remuneration may not be paid to *Nyaya Panchs* but they should be reimbursed travelling and other out of pocket expenses. It is true that there is some loss of earning for the members of the *Nyaya Panchayat*. But it is not so substantial considering the time that they have to devote to *Nyaya Panchayat* work. On the other hand, as elected members of a body administering justice, they enjoy a certain prestige and status. The pride of performing an important service to the community would itself be a reward more important than a small remuneration.

Court Experience

It has often been said that the experience with regular courts located at *tehsil* or district headquarters comes handy to the members of *Nyaya Panchayat* in the performance of their judicial duties. It may be noted that there is a wide divergence in approach, procedures and working between the courts and *Nyaya Panchayats*. It would, therefore, not be desirable to insist on court experience. It may even become counter productive if some of the members of *Nyaya Panchayat* tend to favour formal procedures. It may also be pointed out that more law abiding and non-controversial a member of *Nyaya Panchayat* is, the less likelihood of his exposure to courts. I would lay the greatest emphasis on intensive training of the *Panchs* in the legal and procedural aspects of their work than on exposure to courts of law.

Organizational Membership

"Ordinarily, most of the activities in the *Panchayati Raj*, including that of *Nyaya Panchayat*, are considered an exercise of corporate life and reflected in the association with various social organizations and, therefore, an asset to the members of *Nyaya Panchayat*. On the other hand, the membership of a *Nyaya Panchayat* also acts as a feedback, and leads to enhanced participation in other collective activities."*

However, it is of utmost importance that the members of *Nyaya Panchayat* should be kept away from controversy and extremism which may seriously undermine their work and experience. Another important matter to consider is whether membership of a political party should operate as a bar to fight

---

* M. Z. Khan and Kamlesh Sharma, *Profile of a Nyaya Panchayat*, National Publishing House, New Delhi, 1982.

Nyaya Panchayat elections. The time honoured view is that fighting *Panchayat* elections on party basis would politicise the *Nyaya Panchayats*, thereby, making them less objective. If the *Panchayats* are to be a part of a democratic polity, it is inconceivable that the *Panchayati Raj institutions* could remain insulated from political influence. My feeling is that the background of political parties would enrich the mental equipment of the *Panchs* and give a sharper edge to their social responsibilities. The candidates, whether independent or associated with political parties, would, in any case, be known to the electorate. In the *Panchayat* elections, unlike the elections to state assemblies and parliament, the electorate prefer to vote by and large for candidates for their maturity, character and impartial attitude whatever party they may belong to rather than on party-basis. So, democratic institutions of the *Gram Panchayat* and *Nyaya Panchayats* should not be given an undemocratic complexion.

Tenure

The recent constitutional amendments enjoin an election in *Panchayti Raj institutions* every five years. "A consideration of the tenure of *Nyaya Panchayat* members assumes importance for several reasons. It would show among other things, to what extent the periodical elections for Village *Panchayats* as well as *Nyaya Panchayats* have been punctually held and how far the rules governing the periodicity of elections and term of office of the members have been followed. It may also show the amount of experience members have of serving in *Nyaya Panchayats*. To some extent it may indicate their proficiency and competence in adjudication work. It may also bring out the extent of monopolisation or dispersion of influence, authority or powers, emanating from members of *Panchayats*. Indirectly, it may also tell the extent of popular participation in this area of social activity."* Hithertofore, the term of office of the members of *Nyaya Panchayat* does not show any country-wide uniformity. It is suggested that it should be five years, subject to extension by

* M. Z. Khan and Kamlesh Sharma, *Profile of a Nyaya Panchayat*, National Publishing House, New Delhi, 1982.

competent authority. The term of office of the members of *Nyaya Panchayat* should run concurrent with that of the parent Village *Panchayat*.

Appointment to the Nyaya Panchayat

"The *Nyaya Panchayat* of the ancient times followed the procedure neither of nomination nor of elections for the selection of the members. Those appointed to its office generally used to be persons of prestige, influence and maturity. They largely enjoyed the confidence of the village folk. The proceedings followed in this regard generally used to be informal and based on unanimity."* Presently, the Constitution provides for election to the *Village Panchayats*. How should the *Nyaya Panchayats* be constituted? Whether the *Nyaya Panchayats* should also be elected through a separate process of election or be elected from amongst the elected members, of *Village Panchayats*? In this connection the Study Team of 1962 observed: "As to the method of constitution of *Nyaya Panchayats*, the system of nomination in any form has to be ruled out. Villagers must be given a free hand and the choice as between direct elections and indirect elections. The method of indirect elections seems to offer, for the time being, the best solution and of the various possible methods of indirect election, the best seems to be of the type in which each of the *Gram Panchayats* in the *Nyaya Panchayats* circle elects a specified number of persons to serve on the *Nyaya Panchayats*." I am in total agreement with this proposal and would like to stress that too much emphasis on the method of appointment of the members of the *Nyaya Panchayats* under the present circumstances would not be desirable. It is the human material and the general social environment which make the difference.

The recommendations of the Law Commission envisage that the statutory village level courts, to be called *Gram Nyayalayas*, may be set up for the resolution of disputes in rural areas. Further, that *Gram Nyayalayas* should consist of legally trained

---

* M. Z. Khan and Kamlesh Sharma, *Profile of a Nyaya Panchayat*, National Publishing House, New Delhi, 1982.

judges, who would be presiding judges, alongwith two lay judges. The legally trained judges would belong to the cadre of *Panchayati Raj* judges, to be specifically set up for this purpose, and would ordinarily form part of the subordinate judiciary in the state. Further that the selection of lay judges may be done out of a panel of non-political, well informed and social service-oriented persons of the given area by a selection committee comprising of the district judge and the district magistrate of the concerned district. The lay judges should have a graduate degree as the qualification failing which those who have gained higher secondary school examination certificate should be eligible for selection. Educational qualification may be prescribed as desirable and not as minimum qualification. In the case of persons belonging to SC/ST backward communities and women, the educational qualifications may be dispensed with if adequate number of persons with such qualification are not available. Persons to be selected shall preferably be within the age group 30-65 years.

The Law Commission recommendations, particularly those relating to a judicial officer presiding over the village *nyayalayas* have been supported by some other commissions, and authorities that have gone into the subject. Here it may be emphasised that the present exercise is directed towards the setting up of *Nyaya Panchayats*, rather than village level courts, because of the following reasons:

(i) *Nyaya Panchayats* are rooted in history and tradition in the country and there is a broad degree of acceptance of these institutions among the village people.

(ii) *Nyaya Panchayat* would have better accessibility to the rural poor, illiterate persons and weaker sections of society.

(iii) *Nyaya Panchayat* would be an economical proposition and would not involve substantial expenditure as in the case of the proposed village courts.

(iv) The participatory nature of justice and the involvement of community in judicial administration would be available under the *Nyaya Panchayat* only.

The composition of *Gram Nyayalayas* with a legally trained judge would involve huge cost even if a *Gram Nayalaya* is constituted at the level of a *taluk* or *tehsil*. In a village court, the accent would be on formal procedures and technical and legalistic side of the administration of justice rather than on expeditious resolution of disputes in a simple and informal manner. The legally trained judge would dominate *Gram Nyayalayas* and would inhibit delivery of substantive justice. The proposed arrangement of the *Panchayat* judge being a part of the subordinate judiciary would merely make it one more layer of judiciary without any change in its orientation and style of functioning. The resourceful and dominant sections of society would continue to manipulate even this court for their ends. It would also open up the process of appeal and revision all along the line.

People's participation in village courts on the basis of selection, with whatever safeguards, can never be insulated from social and political pressures. Further, the system of selection does not provide for people's participation in justice. The selected persons are also not accountable to the village community. Thus, the social content in the administration of justice would be missing. The prescription of formal degree or qualification for being selected as lay judges is not desirable because as already stated, this would deprive vast mass of people from any sense of participation in justice administration and this would make judgeship an elitist institution.

Elderly people command greater respect and following because of their maturity, experience, knowledge of local custom and traditions. Therefore age eligibility qualification should start from forty and the age of retirement fixed at 70 years. In case of women and SCs and STs the higher age qualifications could be dispensed with as it may bring in biases against the problems faced by younger women in social relations such as between daughter-in-law and her in-laws or between young women wishing to marry against the wishes of parents, etc.

Training

The successful functioning of *Nyaya Panchayats* will in no small measure depend upon the approach that the members of these organisations bring to bear upon their working. Proper training of the members of the *Nyaya Panchayats* towards cultivating this approach is a *sine qua non.* Such training should comprise like rudimentary knowledge of law, the method of hearing cases, and efforts to bring about conciliation and resolution of disputes by compromise and finally the decision making process. The members of the *Nyaya Panchayats* should in particular be taught that they must conform to the principles of natural justice. Always and at all times justice, equity and good conscience should guide their deliberations and decisions. They should also be advised that whenever possible, endeavour should be made at reconciliation between parties and eradicate the causes of disputes and thus pave the way for better relationships. The training should be short but frequent and should be imparted as far as possible by mobile teams in the rural areas.

Territorial Jurisdiction

The basic problem faced by people in administration of justice is that the courts are located at considerable distance from the villages, the judicial process is time-consuming and dilatory, it is expensive both for the government and the litigants and there is too much emphasis on procedural rather than substantive justice. These problems are not likely to be solved by setting up of *Gram Nyayalayas* at *taluk/tehsil* levels. If justice has to be accessible to the rural poor and the weaker sections on terms they can afford, justice administering institutions must be constituted atleast at the *Panchayat* level if not at the village level. This matter will be discussed in detail later while dealing with the organisational set-up of the *Nyaya Panchayats.*

Civil and Criminal Jurisdiction

The Law Commission emphasised that it has not been able to find any correlation between the pecuniary value of the subject matter of a dispute and the capacity of the judge to deal with it. A lay arbiter chosen by the parties can deal with the subject matter valued at any amount. However, while devising a new forum it is worthwhile to break the tenuous and unscientific connection between the pecuniary value of the subject matter of dispute and the capacity of the person to deal with it. The real correlation should be established keeping in view the nature of the dispute and the capacity of the person charges with the duty to resolve such a dispute. I am in total agreement with the opinion of the Commission that the jurisdiction must be referable to the subject matter of the dispute and not its precuniary value. The conferment of civil jurisdiction on *Nyaya Panchayats*, in respect of disputes covered by the following subjects, is favoured.

1. Civil Disputes

Dispute arising out of the implementation of agrarian reforms and allied statutes for example

(a) Tenancies-protected and concealed and contested
(b) Boundary disputes and encroachments
(c) Right to purchase
(d) Use of common pasture
(e) Entries in revenue records
(f) Regulation and timing of taking water from irrigation channels
(g) Disputes as to assessment of revenue

2. Property Disputes

(a) Village and farm houses (possessions)
(b) Easement: rights of way for men, cart and cattle to fields and courtyards
(c) Water channels
(d) Right to draw water from a common well, and tubewell

3. Family Disputes

(a) Marriage
(b) Divorce
(c) Custody of children
(d) Inheritance and succession-share in property
(e) Maintenance

4. Other Disputes

(a) Nonpayment of wages and violation of Minimum Wages Act
(b) Money suits arising either from trade transactions or money lending
(c) Disputes arising out of the partnership in cultivation of lands
(d) Disputes as to the use of forest produce by local inhabitants
(e) Disputes arising from Bonded Labour System (Abolition) Act 1976 and the Protection of Civil Rights Act

Criminal Jurisdiction

1. At early stages giving the jurisdiction in criminal matters for offences triable by a First Class Judicial Magistrate, is not preferred. In my view the *Nyaya Panchayats* should have the exclusive criminal jurisdiction over the offences enumerated in Appendix I and such other offences under the local and special laws as may be notified by the government subject to the following conditions:

   (i) The information/report/complaint lodged before the *Nyaya Panchayats* is against a specific person/persons.

   (ii) The person against whom the information/report/complaint lodged has not had previous conviction for any one or more offences enumerated in Chapters Twelve and Seventeen of the IPC or under Sections 264, 265, 266, 269, 272 and 273 of the IPC.

(iii) In the case of offences against property the value of property is not more than Rs. 1,000.

(iv) The alleged offences under Sections 172, 173, 174, 175, 177, 178, 179, 180, 182, 186 and 187 of the IPC are relatable to the proceedings by the *Nyaya Panchayats*.

2. *Nyaya Panchayats* shall be competent to take cognizance of offences falling under their jurisdictions on information/report/complaint received by them directly either from the affected parties or otherwise.

3. If an information or complaint invoking an offence falling within the jurisdiction of the *Nyaya Panchayat* is laid before the police they shall transmit it forthwith for disposal by *Nyaya Panchayat* without making an inquiry, except in the circumstances mentioned below.

   (i) On receipt of information/complaint of the nature mentioned above by officer incharge of police station, he may, if considered necessary by him in the interests of public peace, make an immediate inquiry into the matter to ascertain facts thereof. On conclusion of his inquiry if he finds that an offence falling within the jurisdiction of the *Nyaya Panchayat* is made out, he shall submit a brief report indicating the result of his inquiry and the facts thereof to the *Nyaya Panchayat* for further action. If, however, the offence made out falls within the jurisdiction of a regular court, he should deal with it further as required under the CrPC.

Nyaya Panchayat shall not be bound by procedure of the courts or the laws of evidence. Their proceedings shall be in the nature of an inquisitorial inquiry which would mean that the *Nyaya Panchayat* would itself take a positive role in the inquiry to ascertain the facts regarding the involvement, or otherwise, of the person/persons concerned instead of merely functioning as an adjudicating body to give its views on two versions put before it, one by the prosecution and the other by the defence. The new arrangement would confer on the *Nyaya Panchayats* a slightly extended role as compared to the regular courts, in the sense that the *Nyaya Panchayat* would be free to make field inquiries also to ascertain the availability of evidence and witnesses. When the system gets going the *Nyaya Panchayat* may require the assistance of some village-based field staff to make inquiries of this kind.

Parties to the proceedings before the *Nyaya Panchayat* shall not be allowed to be represented by lawyers. Exceptions may arise when a person happens to be arrested or otherwise detained in custody in connection with an offence relating to the proceedings before the *Nyaya Panchayat* in which case the provisions of the article 22(1) of the Constitution may get attracted.

There should be provision to enable a *Nyaya Panchayat* to issue processes to compel appearance of parties before it, when necessary.

If on the facts ascertained in the course of proceedings before the *Nyaya Panchayat* it is found that the case will fall beyond the criminal jurisdiction of the *Nyaya Panchayat*, the *Nyaya Panchayat* shall transfer the case to the court of competent jurisdiction for further proceedings under the CrPC.

The findings of *Nyaya Panchayat* shall be based on the majority view of the competent members. Punishment awarded by a *Nyaya Panchayat* shall be limited to fine not exceeding Rs. 1000. Fines shall be recovered by processes applicable to arrears of land revenue. A *Nyaya Panchayat* shall not be competent to award any sentence of imprisonment even in default of payment of fine.

If in any particular case, having regard to the circumstances thereof, the *Nyaya Panchayat* feels that the person found guilty by it merits more serious punishment than is awardable by it, it shall remit the case to the Chief Judicial Magistrate of the district concerned for further action on the lines indicated in section 325 CrPC.

It is expected that the *Nyaya Panchayat* as proposed would be able to handle a fairly substantial volume of civil and criminal litigation which otherwise would be taken up by regular courts. This alternative mechanism for dealing with routine civil and criminal matters in the rural areas would greatly facilitate quicker disposal in courts, of cases of more serious magnitude. It is also expected that vexatious litigation from rural areas would diminish since villagers who may now be induced to involve their opponents in complaints lodged in distant police stations would be more cautious if their complaints are to come up promptly before a local body. The resultant advantages will be many in the light of overall effect on the administration of justice.

Court Fee

There has been a lively debate whether court fee shall be levied on the proceedings before the *Nyaya Panchayat*.

Various conferences and debates have not revealed a consensus in this behalf. A number of states have in the past strongly opposed the proposal of abolition of court fee. Votaries of abolition contend that court fee is a tax on justice and no civilised society can tax justice. Another view is that an indigent person suffers serious handicap in access to justice by not being able to pay court fees. Keeping aside the wider issue of the jurisdiction or otherwise of levying court fee, it is felt that in respect of proceedings before *Nyaya Panchayat* which will be catering to the needs of the rural poor, the levy of court fee will be anchronistic, while there may be ample jurisdictions of levying court fee, elsewhere. In the proceedings before the *Nyaya Panchayat*, looking to the nature of disputes, the class of litigants, the economic status of the parties ordinarily coming before it, the levy of court fee would be inappropriate.

Provision of Appeal and Revision

According to the Law Commission, it is fallacious to assume that the errors are not committed at higher levels of judiciary. A number of decisions of the Supreme Court can be cited to substantiate the proposition that the decision of trial court which was set aside by the High Court was restored by the Supreme Court. It can, therefore, be said with confidence that a provision for appeal is not a guarantee of justice nor a bulwark against arbitrary or biased decisions.

It is equally true that no one is infallible. "The court of appeal has been described as court of error". Therefore, its jurisdiction has been held to be co-extensive with the trial courts. Experience also teaches us that a forum for appeal cannot necessarily cure all errors. Furthermore, the chances of witnesses committing perjury are far less at the *Nyaya Panchayat* level. By and large most of the facts are already in the notice of some members of *Panchayat* as well as the villagers. Having regard to all these circumstances, it is felt that no appeal shall lie against the decision of *Nyaya Panchayat*. Any provision to the contrary would open up a Pandora's Box.

As advised by the Law Commission a revision petition to correct errors of law which had affected the decision of *Nyaya Panchayat* to the District Court of the district in which *Nyaya Panchayat* is functioning, would meet the requirement. The revising court may correct the errors in a revision petition filed by a party against whom adverse decision is rendered. But if error of law has not substantially affected the decision of the case, the same shall not be interfered with. Even if it comes to the conclusion that another view is possible, it would have no jurisdiction to interfere with the decision of the *Nyaya Panchayat*. This limited revisional jurisdiction should be confined to correct patent errors of law or to prevent miscarriage of justice.

The Law Commission finally advised us "To put the matters beyond the pale of controversy, no revision would be against the decision of the revisional authority or against the decision of the *Nyaya Panchayat* to the High Court under Section 1215 of CrPC or article 227 of the Constitution. Both the jurisdictions will have to be extinguished by appropriate legislation".

The jurisdiction conferred on *Nyaya Panchayat* should be

exclusive to the extent that in respect of matters covered by the jurisdiction conferred on *Nyaya Panchayat* the jurisdiction of any other court is ousted.

At this stage it may be emphasised that the proposed setup of the *Nyaya Panchayats* would be successful only if it is given statutory backing in a new self contained legislation.

Execution

A simple method of execution of the *Nyaya Panchayat* order must be provided for. The nature of execution would depend upon the relief granted by the decision of the *Nyaya Panchayat.* All authorities of revenue department operating at village or *Tehsil* level, all police authorities at both the levels shall be put under obligation to assist the *Nyaya Panchayat* in discharging its functions and performing its duties. Failure on the part of any such authority shall be treated as a misconduct and *Nyaya Panchayat* should be empowered to take effective action against such defaulting authorities.

Administrative Organization

The objective of a proper administrative set-up of a *Nyaya Panchayat* is to ensure its efficient functioning. The efficiency is reflected by its capacity to inspire confidence in the villages, it is intended to serve, by prompt cognizance of complaints referred to it and their speedy disposal in a most dispassionate and objective manner. It should be the endeavour of a *Nyaya Panchayat* to bring about compromise without coercion but through ability to make the contestants realise the virtue of honest conduct and living under conditions of good neighbourliness, understanding and conciliation.

To achieve these objectives the *Nyaya Panchayats* should comprise of a cohesive body of men, not too large in number. If the composition of the *Nyaya Panchayat* is large, it may not always be possible for it to assemble easily at short notice. Moreover, the decision of day-to-day complaints and disputes is best made by a smaller compact body of *Panchs*.

We have already discussed the manner of appointment of members of a *Nyaya Panchayat* through indirect elections. From the organisational point of view, what should be the territorial jurisdiction of a *Nyaya Panchayat*? Should every village have a *Nyaya Panchayat* or should a *Nyaya Panchayat* be constituted for a group of villages? In some parts of the country, a village grows out of one family taking abode in a small area for purposes of cultivation. In other parts, even if a village does not comprise one family yet it is no more than a small hamlet. In my view, an effective administrative set-up can be organised by combining both the territorial and population factors. In this connection, the views of the Congress Village Panchayat Committee of 1954 have been found to be useful. According to the suggestions of this Committee, the composition and functions of the *Nyaya Panchayats* should be separated from *Village Panchayats*. Each *Nyaya Panchayat* should serve a few villages covering a population of about 5-6 thousand in a radius of say, 5 kilometres. Based on the above considerations, I am of the view, that a *Nyaya Panchayat* should serve on an average five villages with a population ranging between 1,500-2,000 souls. Each *Village Panchayat* should elect five persons to serve as members of the *Nyaya Panchayat*. Thus, a *Nyaya Panchayat* should not have more than 25 members. Due regard should be paid to the claims of women and Scheduled Castes and Tribes in the elections to the *Nyaya Panchayat*. Those elected to the *Nyaya Panchayat* should elect from amongst themselves, a *Sarpanch* and an *Upsarpanch* by majority vote. Each *Panch* so elected to the *Nyaya Panchayat* should take oath of office bearing true faith and allegiance to the Constitution and doing right to all manner of people and faithfully discharging his duties as a member of the *Nyaya Panchayat* without fear or favour, affection or ill will.

A member of *Nyaya Panchayat* may submit his resignation to the *Sarpanch* at any time. If a vacancy occurs in the office of a *Panch*, *Sarpanch* or *Upsarpanch* by reason of death, removal or resignation, the vacancy shoud be filled by a fresh election from the village concerned. The *Sarpanch/Upsarpanch* may be elected in the manner mentioned above. However, any person appointed as a *Panch* to the *Nyaya Panchayat* ceases to be a member of the Village *Panchayat* from the day of his appointment.

Having considered the legal, administrative and organisational matters, we now come to the nitty-gritty of the functioning of the *Nyaya Panchayats*. Consequent upon, the constitution of a *Nyaya Panchayat* and the election of the *Sarpanch* and the *Upsarpanch*, the *Sarpanch* should proceed to set-up atleast five panels of *Panchs*, comprising five members each, in a manner that all the constituent villages are represented in every panel. These panels should elect one member from amongst themselves as the presiding *Panch*. The members of these panels should be reshuffled every year so that during five years–the life span of the *Nyaya Panchayat*, the constituent members have an opportunity to serve on all the five panels. The *Sarpanch* and the *Upsarpanch* should head the panels to which they are assigned. Infact, it is the intention that during the course of five years, the *Sarpanch* should have headed all the panels once.

The *Sarpanch* should maintain three registers to record criminal, civil and miscellaneous complaints separately in each register. On receipt of a complaint it should be immediately recorded in the relevant register and referred to a panel for disposal. The presiding *Panch* of the panel should record it in his own register and fix a date for the panel to assemble for the disposal of the complaint. The parties concerned should also be informed accordingly. If it is a criminal complaint, an effort should be made to commence the hearing the very next day. The panel should hear the parties and record such evidence as they adduce or the panel itself desires to call and endeavour to decide the case the same day or the next day. In case of civil or miscellaneous complaints, the panel should assemble not more than three days after the receipt of the complaint and strive to decide it within two days. The panel should record the summary of evidence and its final order giving reasons, in a register to be maintained for the purpose.

The next complaint received by the *Sarpanch* should be forwarded to the second panel and the next to the third panel and so forth. The object of this arrangement is equitable distribution of work amongst all the five panels. Some experts have suggested a periodical meeting of the *Nyaya Panchayats* to take up the complaints referred to them. I am not in favour of the idea of periodical meetings. The chances of resolving the criminal complaints and the recovery and restoration of stolen property, etc. are much brighter with prompt cognizance of the cases. The periodicity principle confers litttle advantage but may account for undue delay and frustration. In criminal cases particularly, it is imperative that the complainant is heard and the accused summoned without undue delay.

The *Sarpanch*, *Upsarpanch* or a *Panch*, should not take part in hearing a case involving themselves, their relatives, employees and business partners or where they are personally interested. The *Nyaya Panchayat* panels should have fixed places at which to conduct their proceedings, preferably in the *Panchayat Ghar* or in some other place which the people could visit, without any let or hinderance. In no case should the sitting of a *Nyaya Panchayat* take place at a private house. As far as possible the cases pertaining to a village must be heard in the village itself.

It is felt that a *Nyaya Panchayat* should be provided with a competent secretary who would not only maintain the record of proceedings but also impart to the *Nyaya Panchayat* a touch of continuity. Depending upon the workload, there may be one secretary for one, two or three *Nyaya Panchayats*. The secretary need not possess legal qualification but must ordinarily be educated upto higher secondary and must be given proper training. An appropriate mechanism should be laid down for the selection of the secretaries keeping strictly in view the principles of decentralization of administration. The secretary should be under the administrative control of the *Sarpanch* and the *Nyaya Panchayat* shall exercise complete disciplinary powers over the secretaries. It is essential that the secretary should give *Nyaya Panchayat* work his undivided attention, keep the records up-to-date, ensure the timely service of summons and keep the accounts in order.

Maintenance of Records

For the effective working of *Nyaya Panchayat* it is necessary to maintain records properly. Based on the experience of working of *Nyaya Panchayats* in several states, the maintenance of following records would seem to be desirable.

1. Register of Criminal Cases
2. Register of Civil Cases
3. Register of Miscellaneous Cases
4. Register of Proceedings
5. Summons Register Cash Book
6. Receipt Register
7. Dispatch Register
8. Stock Register
9. Requests for Copies Register
10. Office and Travelling Expenses Register

At this point, I wish to draw attention to a paper by Mrs. Alice Jacob, member of the Law Commission, presented at a seminar organized by the Institute of Social Sciences, in February 1995. This paper embodies a comprehensive model for a *Nyaya Panchayat*. I attach at Appendix II a copy of this paper.

To sum up, the following essential features would determine the success of the *Nyaya Panchayat*, also the achievement of the ideal of dispensing cheap and quick justice to rural population:

1. The *Nyaya Panchayats* should be a representative body, constituted through a process of election and function in a cohesive manner, with commitment to deliver justice.

2. The elections to *Nyaya Panchayats* should be very regular, otherwise, people tend to lose interest in the electoral process.

3. The *Nyaya Panchs* should be accorded the status and protection due to the members of a body administering justice and should be treated as public servants.

4. All members of the *Nyaya Panchayats* should develop a truly objective approach through intensive training and dispassionate functioning.

5. The decisions of the *Nyaya Panchayats* should inspire confidence in all sections of the village community in general and the feuding parties in particular.

6. Accessibility to the humblest in the village community and giving him the opportunity of being heard in respect of his grievance should be the hall-mark of the success of the *Nyaya Panchayats*. Every single member of the community should feel that justice is being dispensed at the door step.

7. The judgements of the *Nyaya Panchayats* should be delivered after thoroughly sifting the evidence in a speedy manner without causing undue delay and expense to the parties.

8. The *Nyaya Panchayats* must not at any stage give an impression of being influenced by politics of power, pressure groups or vested interests.

9. The *Nyaya Panchayats* should encourage the principle of conciliation as a way of deciding disputes. From the sociological point of view, this method would be of great advantage.

10. For their efficiency as organs administering justice at the grassroots level, it is imperative that the financial conditions of the *Nyaya Panchayats* should be satisfactory.

11. The *Nyaya Panchayats* should receive continuous co-operation from all associated agencies to render their working smooth and efficient.

This model framework, however, is not meant to be rigidly applicable to all states. In our vast country with widely different administrative culture in different states, different historical background, varying size of population, a uniform model cannot be imposed.

Chapter 6

Conclusion

"THE genius of the mature Indian system was that although the government had supervisory power, it did not initiate litigation and did not provide a professional cadre of judges or regular system of appeals. The typical village court contained representatives of all castes and religions. The decisions took long to emerge and made themselves apparent by stages. But the system achieved, even after some generation of conflicts, substantial justice between the actual parties (not merely the ostensible ones). Inquisition was the technique used in criminal matters, matters of state security and where the tranquillity of the tax payer was at risk. The law applied was made up of custom, the religious laws, the *shastras* (the distilled wisdom of many generations of students) and last but not the least, royal regulations and ordinances passed *ad hoc* and of uncertain life. It was only in a very limited range of matters that the ruler took this initiative and exercised this power of inquisition and punishment in public interest as he understood it.

"In the present set-up, revenue laws and land reforms for example, come within the scope of what can be characterised as 'inquisition'. Yet judicial system sticks strangely to the Anglo-American adversary procedures with the judge acting as the unifier. Within the last decade, however, an inquisitional procedure was set up by an amendment of Civil Procedure Code for family cases. One wonders whether this expedient could catch on and spread to other topics. It is not suggested that the review of administrative decisions should be abandoned; the basic notions of parliamentary democracy, unknown to the *shastras* have sunk too deep. But some modification would be accepted, I submit at the village level where respect for honest authoritarianism is far from dead and reminds one of the pre-revolutionary Russia. The conscience of the great ones and the elders is the small man's real security."*

---

* Ram Avtar Sharma, *Justice and Social Order in India,* Intellectual Publishing House. 1984.

This is the spirit in which this chapter for the revival and the revitalisation of *village Nyaya Panchayats* is written. I propose to some practical issues which are worthy of consideration, to make this experiment a success.

A statutory basis for *Nyaya Panchayat* will have to be provided through statewise enactments. In the wake of the 73rd Amendment of the Constitution, practically all state governments have brought state legislations but to the best of my knowledge scarcely any one addressed themselves to decentralisation of the administration of justice. It is indeed questionable whether the intention of the Constitutional amendment was really to bring about decentralization of power. The state legislatures with specific regard to the establishment of *Nyaya Panchayats* will have to define the manner of elections to *Nyaya Panchayats*, the areas of their jurisdiction, lay down qualifications needed for candidates and the periodicity of elections.

The new act would require the selection of a chairman to constitute the benches, define the minimum number of each bench. State governments will have the power to regulate the procedure, the number of sittings by making rules. Every member of *Nyaya Panchayat*, chairman, the officers of the staff of *Nyaya Panchayat* (secretary, peon) would be public servants within the meaning of the IPC and entitled to the protection under the Judicial Officer's Protection Act while acting as members of *Nyaya Panchayat*.

Even at the cost of some duplication, I would like to reiterate that majority of field studies undertaken have revealed that the establishment of *Nyaya Panchayat* have definitely brought about the seal of justice deserved by the people. Justice is no longer being administered for the village folk in the strange atmosphere by a magistrate who does not share most of their value judgements. The justice would administered right at the doorstep by the litigants' kinsmen who are a part of the village community.

As a corollary, the litigant may find it difficult to indulge in any falsehood when justice is being administered by his kinsmen. The village community all over the country has received the concept of *Nyaya Panchayat* well. I hope to dwell briefly on the conditions of the tribal areas which are a further eloquent testimony to this concept.

The institution of *Nyaya Panchayat* has encouraged the principle of reconciliation as a way of deciding the disputes. At whatever stage it is arranged, the method of reconciliation for resolving the village disputes is an advantage from the sociological point of view.

In some states there has been a good deal of criticism on the delay in the disposal of cases by the *Nyaya Panchayat*. Though the delay is distressing and it may lead to accumulation of arrears and even tend to sometimes shake the confidence of villagers. It may, however, be pointed out that these shortcomings are to some extent natural and would be removed as the institution gets firmly rooted in the village and conditions are created to enable its members to feel more interested in the work. It should not be forgotten that the institution has yet to build its traditions with regard to the procedure of work. The facilities for secretarial and clerical assistance have yet to be made available. The situation is bound to improve when this is done.

The problem of executing the *Nyaya Panchayat* decisions is an important one. The *Nyaya Panchayat* depend on an SDO or some other executive functionary for the execution of their decisions. Very often adequate cooperation is not available from these agencies. A mechanism has to be organised for the execution of *Nyaya Panchayat* decisions and decrees by laying down clear cut rules by the state government.

As an institution, the *Nyaya Panchayat* commands both prestige and confidence of the villagers. The defects and shortcomings are largely administrative and procedural and can easily be remedied. Efforts should be made to see that the administration including financial, of the *Nyaya Panchayats* is streamlined to give it strength to sustain the confidence the people have reposed in them. Extra care needs to be taken to ensure that politics of power which has started vitiating the *Panchayati Raj institutions*, does not effect *Nyaya Panchayats*. When judicial and *Nyaya Panchayat*s were combined the chances of politics corrupting judicial process were far greater than when *Nyaya Panchayats* are intend to function as custodians of justice.

The working of *Nyaya Panchayat*s suffers when the state governments refuse to hold elections regularly. The elections to *Nyaya Panchayat* must be held with meticulous regularity. After the elections the training of *Panchs* should receive the highest priority. The training is not a one shot exercise and should be a continuous process. Mobile teams should be organised to tour the rural areas to keep the knowledge of the *Panchs* in trim and indulge in a healthy educative dialogue. Simple manuals and handbooks should be available for reference purposes. It should be incumbent on all *Panchs* to attend the training sessions.

There has to be sufficient amount of political will to devise a new form of decentralisation in India. When a new legislations is brought on the statute book, it is for people to operate on the ground in *mandal* or *Gram Sabha*. We need an absolutely new legislative approach where legal language and drafting should be far simpler. It is possible to write simpler and briefer laws which can communicate and help people.

Further the legislation should not merely indicate devolution but embrace the overall scheme. There should be real sharing of power rather than mere delegation. If there is only a tendency to avoid national courts from getting clogged, with problems that are small, petty and localised, the idea is not to democratise judicial administration and not promote greater access to justice, but the idea is to unblock the arteries of the major institutions of the judiciary. This would be of no major consequence. Unless substantial civil and criminal jurisdiction is given to *Nyaya Panchayats*, they would not be able to render participative justice.

Appendices

Appendix I

Criminal Offences over which the *Nyaya Panchayats* will have exclusive jurisdiction:

1. **Indian Penal Code**

Sections 140, 160, 171, 172, 173, 174, 175, 177, 178, 179, 180, 182, 186, 187, 26, 272, 273, 277, 278, 279, 280, 283, 285, 289, 290, 294, 323, 324, 334, 336, 341, 352, 357, 358, 379, 380, 381, 403, 411, 417, 426, 427, 428, 430, 431, 447, 448, 491, 504, 506 (A), 508, 509, 510, 511.

2. **Cattle Trespass Act**

Sections 24, 26

3. **Public Gambling Act**

Sections 3, 4, 7, 13

4. Any other offences under local and special Acts in respect of which the State Government confer the power through a special notification.

Appendix II

Rural Litigation: Role of Nyaya Panchayats as Agents of Grassroots Justice

Alice Jacob
Member, Law Commission,
Former Director,
Indian Law Institute, New Delhi.

In India many of the existing state legislations on *Panchayati Raj* provide for some form of adjudicatory bodies by whatever name they may be described. These fora for resolution of disputes with people's participation in the administration of justice is the constitutional goal mandated by Article 39A of the Constitution. Article 39A directs the State to secure that the operation of the legal system promotes justice, on the basis of equal opportunity, and shall, in particular, provide free legal aid, by suitable legislation or schemes or in any other way, to ensure that opportunities for securing justice are not denied to any citizen on the ground of economic or other disabilities. The Constitution now mandates us to remove impediments to access to justice in a systematic manner. Article 40 and Articles 243 to 2430 have to be interpreted afresh in the light of the mandate in Article 39A.

In the past, in the organisation of *Nyaya Panchayats*, the predominant consideration had been to reduce the burden on the State court system and not so much as to prevent denial of justice because of economic and other disabilities. The "other disabilities" referred to in Article 39A as distinct from the economic disabilities are those which arise from the profiles of the Indian legal system because of absence of suitable local grassroots organs for handling disputes and emphasis on professionalised justice. Professionalised justice, with lawyers dominating the process of the justice-delivery system, cannot be extended to the bulk of the people in the rural areas because most of the 250,000 lawyers are concentrated in urban areas. Moreover, given the voluntary nature of the profession, they cannot be dispersed adequately and equitably to serve the needs of the masses.

New people's courts or tribunals–not merely procedural alterations–are envisaged in Article 39A to ensure a new legal system and procedure which is operationally geared to social justice and elimination of all disabilities of the masses in getting real, remedial justice. Self-government envisaged by the Constitution must include judicial powers too and that is the rationale for *Nyaya Panchayats* which implies judicial decentralisation at the people's level. Effective access to justice may be seen as the most basic requirement, the most basic human right, of a system which purports to guarantee legal rights.

These judicial institutions represent the secular, equalitarian, modernistic legal ideology for assisting the desired social change. The Law Commission in its Fourteenth Report stresses the "educative value of *Nyaya Panchayats*", just as the Village *Panchayats* would educate the villager in the art of self-government, "so would *Nyaya Panchayats*" train him in the art of doing justice between, fellow citizens and instill in him a growing sense of fairness and responsibility. In this respect, *Nyaya Panchayats* constitute an aspect of overall development.

These *Nyaya Panchayats* constitute a sub-system of the state administration of justice as well as a sub-system of *Panchayats*. For example, in relation to Constitution, finances and secretariat, they constitute a sub-system of Panchayats; in their actual operation they are a sub-system of the state apparatus of justice.

These institutions represent the extension of the state's legal system in the rural areas. The extension of state law means extension of the political system as well. This is sought to be done through structuring *Nyaya Panchayats* in such a manner as would combine some features, for example, formal principles of organisation and operation, hierarchy, oversight and control of the state legal system, with some other prominent features of community dispute-handling processes (e.g. informality, flexibility), etc. This makes these institutions half-way institutions between state judicial institutions on the one hand and those judicial institutions which flourish under the auspices of the communities themselves without the aid of law or state, on the other.

II

The existing system of *Nyaya Panchayats* suffers from a number of shortcomings. These are:

(i) *Nyaya Panchayats* do not have exclusive jurisdiction of civil and criminal cases even within their limited sphere. Their jurisdiction generally is concurrent. Therefore, often proceedings in the *Nyaya Panchayats* are stayed by the higher courts if parties approach them. In effect, *Nyaya Panchayats* can only decide cases in which parties arrive at compromise.

(ii) Very often, *Nyaya Panchayats* do not have power to enforce their decisions. They could not even issue notice and collect fines, etc. *Nyaya Panchayats* suffer from lack of infrastructure facilities like office, staff, stationery, etc.

(iii) Through procedures in the *Nyaya Panchayats* are supposed to be informal, lawyers are not debarred from appearing. With lawyers arguing cases, the procedures become complicated and the advantage of cases being settled quickly and informally gets defeated.

(iv) As pointed out earlier, the jurisdiction of these *Nyaya Panchayats* is very limited. They often decide only minor cases like easement rights, *abadi* disputes, mutation cases, etc. Even minor offences of various departmental laws like forest, electricity, etc. are not within the purview of *Nyaya Panchayats*. Their effectiveness is found to be minimal.

One significant criticism about *Nyaya Panchayats* is that persons rendering justice at this level are without legal training. Villagers are often faction ridden and *Nyaya Panchayats* in that background are, it is claimed, not able to render justice that is free from bias. The greatest criticism is that *Panchayats* and, by the same token, *Nyaya Panchayats* are composed of members who belong to rural elite in the village and the poor and oppressed do not get justice at their hands.

The working of *Nyaya Panchayats* has been examined in detail by the Law Commission in their 114th Report on *Gram Nyayalayas*. The Law Commission has recommended setting up of *Gram Nyayalayas* with the following broad features:

(i) A munsif or civil judge should preside over the *Nyaya Panchayats*. They would be subject to the jurisdiction of High Courts.

(ii) To provide effective people's participation in the administration of justice, the district magistrate and the district and sessions judge for each district should draw up a panel of laymen from respectable residents in the villages having educational attainments, preferably upto a university degree or at least a higher secondary school. In order to ensure that marginal farmers, farm workers, etc. get their due share in the panel, if need arises, educational qualifications may be relaxed in their case. Depending upon the size of each taluka, the list of panelists may vary from 10 to 20. The list should be approved by the High Court.

(iii) Whenever a dispute is brought to the *Panchayat* judge having his headquarters at the taluks level, he would proceed to select two from the panel of laymen, keeping in view the fact that they must be as far as possible from the geographical location of the dispute. The *Panchayat* judge and the two members of the panel will constitute a *Nyaya Panchayat* for the dispute. Such composition would ensure legal expertise and people's participation and would avoid caste, communal and political contamination.

(iv) A major departure of the Law Commission recommendation from the existing *Nyaya Panchayat* is that there is no elective element in it.

III

One view is that while the Law Commission's recommendation tries to provide the element of judifically trained persons to decide cases at the village level, the involvement of judicial officers will make the system totally alien to the *Nyaya Panchayat* system. It will also make the system more formalistic and may not serve the purpose of quick and informal justice at the local level, which is the essence of the *Nyaya Panchayat* system. For the revitalisation of *Nyaya Panchayats*, the following suggestions regarding constitution, composition, jurisdiction and procedure of *Nyaya Panchayats* and appeal and revision from their decisions, respectively are offered for consideration.

A. Constitution of Nyaya Panchayats

Nyaya Panchayats should be completely distinct from *Gram Panchayats*. A person should not be permitted to be elected to both the *Gram Panchayat* and the *Nyaya Panchayats* should not be entitled to seek election to the other.

A *Nyaya Panchayat* should have nine members of which two must belong to scheduled castes and tribes and two should be women.

The constituencies to be delimited for the purpose of *Gram Panchayat* should serve for election to the *Nyaya Panchayat* also.

All members of the *Nyaya Panchayat* should be directly elected by eligible voters of the constituency. Qualifications and disqualifications of membership of *Nyaya Panchayat* should be the same as exist in respect of the *Gram Panchayat* membership.

The minimum age for members of *Nyaya Panchayat* should, however, be 40 years.

No educational qualifications are recommended for election to *Nyaya Panchayats*. What is required in them is their acceptability to all sections, honesty and integrity. The difficulties in the matter of recording evidence, etc. can be overcome by providing secretarial assistance to the *Nyaya Panchayats*. However, the chairman of the *Nyaya Panchayat* should have minimum educational qualifications so that he can record evidence and pass necessary orders himself. The ability to write and read is, therefore, prescribed only for the chairman, without however mentioning specifically any degree, etc.

The term of office of *Nyaya Panchayat* should be the same as that of *Gram Panchayat* so that elections can be conducted at the same time without leading to double expenditure.

A member of *Nyaya Panchayat* who does not attend three meetings consecutively, would automatically lose his membership. The election of a member against a vacancy caused must be carried out within a period of three months.

Nomination or co-option in whatever form should not be allowed in *Nyaya Panchayats*.

B. Jurisdiction of Nyaya Panchayats

The jurisdiction of *Nyaya Panchayat* should extend to all such matters as can be conveniently decided at the *Panchayat* level. It should include matters relating to criminal, civil, revenue, matrimonial, forest, excise and various other central and state laws on cattle trespass, vaccination, prevention of cruelty to animals, electricity, irrigation public gambling, etc.

However, the *Nyaya Panchayats* should be vested with powers to impose a sentence of imprisonment, even for default for payment of fine.

Jurisdiction of *Nyaya Panchayats* relating to criminal, civil and other matters should be exclusive and not concurrent with that of other judicial institutions.

All members of *Nyaya Panchayat* should be deemed to be public servants, within the meaning of Section 21 of the Indian Penal Code, 1860. The provisions of Judicial Officers Protection Act, 1850 should also be applicable to *Nyaya Panchayats*.

Nyaya Panchayat members may be empowered to initiate conciliation proceedings for dispute resolution before the process of adjudication commences. Conciliation as a technique of resolving disputes needs to be encouraged.

For disposal of matters a Bench may consist of five members of *Nyaya Panchayat* of whom one must be from scheduled castes and scheduled tribes and should be a woman. However, in respect of matters involving scheduled castes and scheduled tribes, both members of these communities should be on the Bench. Similarly, on matters involving women, both women members should be on the Bench. There should also be a provision for Full Bench which should consist of all the members of the *Nyaya Panchayat*. Complicated and controversial matters can be decided by the Full Bench.

C. Procedure

The procedure of disposal of matters coming before the *Nyaya Panchayat* should be as simple as possible. Therefore, procedural provisions of the Code of Criminal Procedure, the Code of Civil Procedure, the Evidence Act, the Limitation Act, etc. should not apply to proceedings before *Nyaya Panchayats*. Whatever minimum procedure is expected to be followed should be laid down in the rules and manuals may be framed for this purpose to provide guidance to the members of *Nyaya Panchayats*. The basic principles of natural justice should be observed which should require that no matter should be disposed of in the absence of the concerned parties.

In order to secure the attendance of the accused before *Nyaya Panchayats*, the latter should be empowered to nominate persons who would execute their orders and decrees, and such persons should be conferred powers of police under the Police Acts. Where the accused person fails to appear, despite the efforts of the *Panchayat*, assistance may be taken of the law and order machinery for this purpose.

No court fee or stamp fee should be levied for taking a matter to the *Nyaya Panchayat.*

No legal practitioner should be allowed to appear before the *Nyaya Panchayat.*

All matters entrusted to the *Nyaya Panchayat* should be disposed of in one hearing and on the same day as far as possible in order that speedy justice is delivered and manipulation is avoided. However, where it is unavoidable, reasons for adjournment of hearing should be recorded. But the matter should be disposed of in the second hearing positively.

Nyaya Panchayat should have powers to record first information reports on complaints pertaining to their jurisdiction and forward them to the competent authority thereafter.

A brief record of evidence of each witness appearing should be kept by the *Nyaya Panchayat* and judgement of the *Nyaya Panchayat* should contain reasons. Proceedings of *Nyaya Panchayats* should be in the local language.

Records of *Nyaya Panchayat* should be maintained as per prescribed guidelines. *Nyaya Panchayats* may be provided with secretarial assistance for discharging functions purely of a clerical and routine nature. Complaints may be filed before the *Nyaya Panchayat* orally or in writing.

A comprehensive programme of training of members of *Nyaya Panchayat* on a continuing basis should be carried out.

D. **Appeal and Revision**

There should be a forum of appeal against the orders of *Nyaya Panchayats*. The appellate forum should preferably be at the level of taluk or tehsil or sub-division.

The appellate structure should have the same character as that of the *Nyaya Panchayat*. It should consist of fifteen members, who may be elected by an electoral college consisting of members of *Nyaya Panchayats*. The secretary of this appellate *Panchayat* should be a judicial officer of the rank of munsif to provide guidance on legal aspects.

For disposal of matters at the appellate level, Benches would be constituted of not more than five members. Each time a matter is referred to in appeal, the members serving on the Bench would be required to visit the village of dispute, hold meetings and decide on the spot. The local district/sub-divisional administration should provide conveyance facilities to them for this purpose.

The Manual on *Nyaya Panchayats* should contain detailed guidelines about the jurisdiction, procedure and manner of functioning of appellate *Panchayats*.

In order to curb litigation and make a *Nyaya Panchayats* effective, there should be no revision against the orders of appellate *Panchayats* except in a small number of complicated cases. The revision authority should be district judge/additional district judge at the district level.

The appellate *Nyaya Panchayat* should have powers to transfer cases from one particular *Nyaya Panchayat* to another.

IV

Panchayati Raj institutions in India received a fillip by the enactment of the Constitution (Seventy-third Amendment) Act, 1992. It came into force on 23 April 1993. Its main focus is on promoting self-governance at the grassroot level in the villages in tune with the Directive Principle enshrined in Article 40 of the Constitution. This provision directs the State to take steps to organise *Village Panchayats* and endow them with such powers and authority as to enable them to function as units of self-government. The Amendment incorporated a new part, namely part IX of the Constitution, with a series of articles (Article 243 to Article 2430) making it obligatory for all large states (with a population exceeding 20 lakhs) to set up a three-tier system at the district, intermediate and village levels, providing for their elections every five years or within six months of the *Panchayats* ceasing to exist by supersession or dissolution, laying down for reservation of seats for women, scheduled castes and scheduled tribes and ensuring availability of resources to them by setting up a Finance Commission for quinquennial division of resources between the *Panchayats* and the states.

The Amendment also contains a list of 29 subjects in the Eleventh Schedule which the States may transfer to *Panchayats*. These include, among others, land improvement, land reforms, primary and secondary education, women and child development, poverty alleviation programmes, small scale industries, social and farm forestry, minor irrigation, etc. But this is only a recommendatory provision and not a mandatory one.

All states, to which this amendment is applicable, have brought their laws on *Panchayats* into conformity with the constitutional provisions within the stipulated period of one year.

The Amendment was made with a view to incorporating certain basic features of *Panchayati* governance. It is an instrument of empowerment of these institutions to enable them to function as effective village democracies. However, the Amendment is silent on their role as adjudicatory bodies or rural dispute resolution for delivering speedy and inexpensive justice to the rural populace of India.

When the Constitution Amendment bill was referred to the Joint Committee, the majority of the Committee members felt that there was no need to incorporate a specific provision on *Nyaya Panchayats* as the original bill did not contain one. This led to one member, Bhogendra Jha, to record a minute of dissent. He observed:

> It is well known that in the institutionalised system of dispensation of justice the poor are at the great disadvantage. The system of institution and adjudication of cases in Courts which are far out of the reach of poor villagers, makes this elaborate set up a matter of unattainable luxury for the poor people. The situation cries out for urgent remedial action and it is incumbent on us, charged as we are with the responsibility of laying down a framework of effective *Panchayati Raj* institution in the country, to suggest corrective action in this regard.

The commission of legal policy planners to incorporate the concept of *Nyaya Panchayat* seems to be a conscious one. It was the shared view of the draftsman of the Constitution Amendment that Part IX should not deal with the question of settlement of disputes in the rural areas. The question of rural litigation was left to be dealt with as an integral part of the system of justice for settlement of disputes in general.

The reason is that the tract record of *Nyaya Panchayats* as agent for speedy and inexpensive justice-delivery system in the rural areas has been disappointing. State practice with regard to resolution of rural disputes does not appear to be uniform.

States such as Andhra Pradesh, Maharashtra, Karnataka, Jammu and Kashmir, Kerala and West Bengal have made legal provisions for *Nyaya Panchayats* but these have not been constituted. Laws have not been enforced. Where laws are enforced, as in Bihar, Gujarat, Haryana, Himachal Pradesh, Manipur, Mizoram, Punjab, Uttar Pradesh, Rajasthan, Sikkim, Madhya Pradesh and Orissa, *Nyaya Panchayats* are, for the most part, not functional. The present scenario seems to be that *Nyaya Panchayats* have not established themselves as effective instruments for settlement of disputes.

The gap between the ideal and the ground reality has to be bridged and ways and means have to be found to provide the rural population access to speedy and inexpensive justice. Current thinking seems to be to extend the formal legal system and institutions more effectively to the rural areas and make available the same quality of justice available in urban areas to rural areas as well. Some states such as Karnataka and Madhya Pradesh have adopted pilot projects in some districts with a view to adjudicating cases in the rural sector speedily. Under the Karnataka model, which came into effect in April, 1993, special judicial magistrates adjudicate rural cases at the spot of the dispute, on holidays and beyond the regular court hours. This has resulted in liquidating of about 40 per cent of rural litigation within a period of one year. A similar scheme in Madhya Pradesh commenced in November 1994. Himachal Pradesh has been successfully implementing conciliation process as a dispute resolution mechanism by courts prior to adjudications. In Himachal Pradesh judges visit rural areas for adjudication of disputes. Recent experiments in these states seem to reinforce the view that, given adequate infrastructural facilities, motivation and incentives to judges, courts would be in a position to expedite settlement of rural cases.

V

Revitalisation of *Panchayati Raj* institutions in the country may in course of time, revitalise *Nyaya Panchayats*, which are as present in a moribund state. The concept of people's courts in the form of *Nyaya Panchayats* should not be given up. But to make access to justice to rural populace meaningful, effective extension of the formal court system could be supplemented profitably by *Nyaya Panchayats* as well as by *Lok Adalats*.

References

Alice Jacob and M. C. Mehta, "Panchayati Adalats in the Jammu and Kashmir Legislation" in George Mathew (ed.) *Panchayati Raj in Jammu and Kashmir* (Institute of Social Sciences, New Delhi, 1990).

Cappelletti, Mauro and Garth, Bryant, (ed.) *Access to Justice* (4 volumes) 1978-79.

Government of India, *Report of the Study Team of Nyaya Panchayats* (1962)

Justice V. R. Krishna Iyer, *Our Courts on Trial* (BRPC, Delhi, 1987).

Report of the Joint Committee *on the Constitution* (*Seventy-second Amendment*) *Bill 1991*, see Gazette of India Extra-ordinary, Part-II, Section II, dated 14.07.1992, 3 at 10.

The Law Commission of India, One Hundred and Fourteenth Report on *Gram Nyayalayas* (1986).

The Law Commission of India, (Fourteenth *Report on Reform of Judicial Administration* (1958).

Upendra Baxi, "Access, Development and Distributive Justice", Vol. 18, *Journal of the Indian Law Institute* (JILI) 375 (1976).

Bibliography

Agarwala, B.R. *Our Judiciary*, New Delhi, National Book Trust, 1993.

Amitava Mukherjee (ed.), *Decentralisation - Panchayats in the Nineties*, New Delhi, Vikas, 1994.

A New Framework for Local Justice presented to Parliament by command of Her Majesty, London, February 1992.

Bhagwati, P.N. *Nyaya Panchayats and Law Nyayalayas* report on National Judicare.

Bhatia, K.L. *Judicial Activism and Social change*, Deep and Deep Publications, New Delhi, 1990.

George Mathew,(ed.), *Status of Panchayati Raj in the States of India, 1994*, Concept Publishing Co., and Institute of Social Sciences, New Delhi, 1994.

Gujarat Committee Report on Legal Aid, Government Press, Gandhi Nagar, 1971.

Khan, M.Z. and Kamlesh Sharma, *Profile of a Nyaya Panchayat*, National Publishing House, New Delhi 1982.

Krishna Iyer V.R. *Of Law and Life*, Vikas, New Delhi,1979.

Kushawaha, R. *Working of Nyaya Panchayat in India*, A case study of Varnasi, Young Asia, New Delhi, 1977.

Law Commission of India, *14th report on Reform of Judicial Administration*, Ministry of Law, Government of India, New Delhi, 1955.

Law Commission of India, *114th report Gram Nyayalayas*, Ministry of Law, Government of India, New Delhi, 1986.

Malcolm S.Adiseshiah... [et al], *Decentralised Planning and Panchayati Raj*, Concept Publishing Co., and Institute of Social Sciences, New Delhi, 1994.

Ram Avtar Sharma, *Justice and Social Order in India*, Intellectual Publishing House, New Delhi, 1984.

Report of the Committee on Panchayati Raj Institutions (Chairman: Shri Asoka Mehta) Ministry of Agriculture and irrigation department of Rural Development, Government of India, New Delhi, August 1978.

Report of a Study Team on Panchayat courts (G.R. Rajagopaul), Ministry of Law, Government of India, New Delhi 1962.

Report of Expert committee on Legal Aid, Processual Justice to the People, (V.R. Krishna Iyer), Government of India, New Delhi, 1971.

Report of National Police Commission (Chairman: Dharm Vira), Government of India, New Delhi, 1976-78.

Richard L. Abel,(ed), *The Politics of Informal Justice*, Vol. 2, School of Law, University of California, Los Angeles.

Roy Burman, B. K. *Indigenous and Tribal People*, Mittal Publications, New Delhi, 1994.

Verghese, J.P. *Empowering the villagers with a dispute settlement system*. (mimeo)

Vidhya Sagar Sharma, *The Panchayat Justice*, Vidya Mandir Publications.

Index